"We are all in this together. And together, we can keep changing the story—for the animals who rely on our care, the people whose lives we touch, and the generations who will carry this work forward. Because a life rooted in compassion and purpose does more than meet the moment—it leaves a legacy that endures."

Cathy M. Rosenthal

Humane Perspectives: Leadership in Animal Welfare

Pet Pundit® Publishing

Published by
Pet Pundit Publishing
Kerrville, Texas
www.CathyRosenthal.com

Front cover design by Cathy M. Rosenthal and Evelina Garliauskiene

Back cover design by Evelina Garliauskiene

Interior layout and design by Evelina Garliauskiene

Edited and curated by Cathy M. Rosenthal

Proofreading services by Jamie Canfield

ISBN: 978-1-948444-03-3

First Edition

For more resources, downloadable templates, and training materials, visit: ***www.CathyRosenthal.com***

Humane Perspectives:

Leadership in Animal Welfare

Foreword by
Jim Tedford, CAWA

Edited and Curated by
Cathy M. Rosenthal, CHES

Table of Contents

Acknowledgments

First and foremost, thank you to all the leaders who contributed to this book. Each of you opened your hearts and shared your stories with honesty, vulnerability, and courage. Your words remind us that leadership in animal welfare isn't about titles. It's about perseverance, compassion, and the ability to inspire others to do better for animals and the people who love them. I am honored to have helped bring your voices together in one place.

To **Jim Tedford**, thank you for your kind and generous foreword, and for your lifelong leadership in our field. You have been one of the most respected voices in animal welfare for decades. Your insight and perspective remind us that progress doesn't happen by chance; it happens when compassion, collaboration, and courage come together. I am deeply honored to have your words open this book.

My deepest thanks to a few leaders who are not only featured in the book, but who took the time to review all these essays prior to publication: **Bonney Brown**, **Jordan Craig**, **Susana Della Maddalena**, and **Rick DuCharme**. Your thoughtful input, insightful questions, and constructive feedback helped shape this book into its final form. It is stronger, clearer, and more meaningful because of your generosity in sharing your time, experience, and expertise.

To **Carol Moulton**, a longtime mentor whose wisdom, guidance, and friendship have profoundly shaped my career. You have been a trusted sounding board, a steady voice of reason, and a source of encouragement through every new challenge and opportunity I have faced. I am endlessly grateful for your friendship, your belief in me, and the many ways you've helped me grow, both as a professional and as a person.

To my son, **Elliott**, who has grown into a remarkable leader in his own right. You inspire me every day with your empathy, creativity, and quiet strength. Watching you find your purpose has been one of the greatest joys of my life. I am endlessly proud of the man you've become; your heart, your kindness, and your integrity shine in everything you do.

To my mom, **Karen**, who showed me how to play basketball by helping me imagine making a free throw over and over again in my mind first. You remind me that anything is possible when you can first see yourself doing it.

To my husband, **Stephen**—thank you for your generosity, patience, and unwavering belief in me. You've kept me grounded and laughing through long days and even longer nights immersed in this work. Your quiet strength, steady encouragement, and faith in what I do have meant more than words can express. You've given me the space to explore my passion and supported it with love and grace, and for that, I am forever grateful.

Finally, **to those in the animal welfare field**—whether staff, volunteer, board member, or donor—thank you for your unwavering compassion, resilience, and commitment to this cause. Your dedication to animal welfare continues to shape a kinder, more humane world—one built on empathy, action, and hope for every living being. You are the heartbeat of this movement.

Cathy M. Rosenthal
Editor and Curator,
Humane Perspectives: Leadership Voices in Animal Welfare

The Leaders Who Changed the Story

When I first ventured into the world, I had two possible careers in mind: veterinarian or writer. I didn't yet realize that life would lead me to a path that blended both—using words and stories to help animals. Like many people at the start of their careers, I was simply searching for work that mattered. I began as a veterinary assistant but, with a background in journalism, photography, and copywriting, also found myself working in newsrooms, advertising agencies, and corporate marketing departments. In time, those seemingly separate worlds converged, each one teaching me something new about people, communication, and purpose—and ultimately creating what I consider the perfect role for me in the animal welfare field—an animal writer and educator.

I arrived at this realization the year my family moved to Indianapolis, Indiana. Once settled, I dropped off résumés at local businesses and organizations, hoping to pick up some contract work writing press releases, radio ads, and marketing copy. One of those résumés landed at the Indianapolis Humane Society (now known as IndyHumane). *What a great place to use my skills and help animals*, I thought. Instead of contract work, though, they offered me a job as public relations manager—and I'm not exaggerating when I say it came with the worst pay I had ever received. Even so, I dropped every other contract and accepted the position without hesitation. Like many who stumble into this profession, my heart just knew it was the right place to be. What I didn't know was that I was stepping into a world filled with both heartbreak and hope.

Back then, animal sheltering was a very different world. Rescue groups were few and far between, foster-care programs were just starting to emerge, transport partnerships were uncommon, large-scale community-cat initiatives and spay/neuter clinic networks were virtually nonexistent, and the idea of a national no-kill conversation had hardly taken shape yet. And social media? Hard to believe since it's such a big part of our lives today, but it simply didn't exist.

What did exist—heartbreakingly—was the reality that millions of healthy, adoptable dogs and cats were being euthanized every year. At the peak of this crisis, national euthanasia estimates reached into the tens of millions of dogs and cats. It was, in many ways, the dark ages for animal welfare.

And yet, even in those difficult early years, extraordinary things were beginning to happen. Passionate people across the country were standing up and daring to imagine something better for dogs and cats. I felt privileged to be a small part of that shift. I served on a committee of national animal-welfare organizations that collaborated to develop the cruelty-free label we still see on products today and advocated for and helped pass legislation that allowed pets in senior-subsidized housing. I was at the forefront of the national effort to spotlight the link between animal cruelty and child abuse, and organized national animal welfare conferences that brought together emerging leaders and new ideas.

As my work evolved from public relations into fundraising, humane education, development, and special events, I watched our field grow and evolve as well. I worked at both the local and national levels, and at every step I met remarkable people whose creativity and determination transformed animal welfare from a quiet, behind-the-scenes effort into a coordinated movement for change. Together, they built the foundation for programs we now take for granted today, like foster care, community cat initiatives, transport collaborations, public sterilization campaigns, and countless other programs born from the belief that we could, and must, do better for animals.

Today, we are saving lives on a scale once thought impossible. Shelters, rescues, veterinarians, and volunteers across the country now work hand in hand to give every animal a chance. This progress didn't happen by chance; it happened because people refused to accept the status quo. They stood up, spoke out, and reimagined what animal welfare could be—and then they made it real.

This book is about those amazing leaders.

For a time, I thought I might become one of them. When the San Antonio Humane Society's executive director left, I was asked to step in as Interim Executive Director. "Isn't this the natural next step for you?" many asked. But it wasn't for me. While I proudly served for almost a year, I knew from the start that leading people wasn't my true calling.

Storytelling was—and remains—my place in this movement. As a former journalist, I have always found joy in writing, connecting, and sharing what was happening in the field. I never needed to be at the top of the organizational chart to feel successful. I just needed to be where I could make the most meaningful contribution—helping others tell their stories, raising awareness, building programs, and encouraging the next generation of changemakers.

Which is why *Humane Perspectives* means so much to me.

This book was created to highlight the stories of some of the most influential, dedicated, and visionary leaders in our field. Their stories are honest, powerful, and full of the kinds of insights you won't find in a textbook or leadership seminar. **This book isn't about debating philosophies or spotlighting which approach has made the greatest impact. We've had those conversations—and while they matter, this book is about something else.** It's about grit, creativity, resilience, and heart. It's about how leaders grow, stumble, get back up, and keep going for the animals and people who need them. *Humane Perspectives* was created to celebrate these leaders, share their lessons from the field, and inspire a stronger, more connected community of people who lead with heart and purpose.

As I read through these essays, I was struck by the remarkable parallels in each leader's journey—stories of discovery, resilience, and purpose unfolding in unique yet familiar ways. I laughed out loud at how many times someone said, *"I didn't mean to go into this work."* And yet here they are—leading, innovating, and shaping the future of animal welfare. It just goes to show that sometimes, we don't choose this work; much like a stray cat looking for a home, the work chooses us.

Whether you're new to animal welfare or have spent decades in this work, I hope you'll find connection and encouragement in this book. If you're a leader, thank you for stepping up and putting in the long hours it takes to do this work. And if you're still finding your place in the field, take comfort in knowing there's no one right path. Your passion—whatever it looks like—is needed, as these leaders so clearly demonstrate in their stories.

To the leaders featured in this book, thank you for sharing your journey. You are among the very best in the animal welfare field—directors, executive directors, CEOs, and visionaries. Thank you for changing the lives of animals and the people who love them. Thank you for sharing your wisdom, your struggles, and your triumphs so openly. And thank you for reminding us that leadership doesn't always mean having all the answers—it means having the courage to keep showing up, to innovate, and to inspire others to follow.

I am also deeply grateful to **Jim Tedford** for his kind and thoughtful foreword. His decades of leadership and advocacy have helped shape the very movement this book celebrates, and his opening words remind us why humane leadership matters now more than ever. His perspective offers both a compass and a challenge—to carry forward the same empathy, integrity, and courage that have shaped this field and will define its future. Thank you for being the voice that reminds us where we've been, and the inspiration that helps lead us to what's next.

If you already work in animal welfare, I'm going to state something you already know: this is one of the hardest jobs on the planet. The hours are long, the heartbreak is real, and public criticism can be relentless. Yet despite all of that, the leaders in this book—and you, perhaps—keep showing up. Day after day, you hold precious lives in your hands, not just because the animals need you, but because compassion keeps calling you to make the world a little kinder.

If you're thinking about joining the animal welfare field, we need you, whether as a professional in the field or as a volunteer, foster caregiver, community cat trapper, advocate, educator, or donor. Every role matters. Every act of kindness makes a difference.

To the next generation of humane leadership, please know that you stand among passionate, dedicated people who have walked similar paths, weathered similar storms, and kept going. Let their stories be the hand on your shoulder, the spark in your next idea, and the quiet reminder that even on the hardest days, you are not alone. As you turn these pages, may these stories remind you that you belong to a community bound by purpose and heart.

We are all in this together. And together, we can keep changing the story—for the animals who rely on our care, the people whose lives we touch, and the generations who will carry this work forward. Because a life rooted in compassion and purpose does more than meet the moment—it leaves a legacy that endures.

Jim Tedford

One Story, One Leader, One Lesson at a Time

I have been involved in the animal welfare profession for over 40 years. But let me be clear—this is not a tale of *"back in my day..."* History is important, not for nostalgia's sake, but because it serves as both a measuring stick and a reminder. It shows us how far we've come, honors those who paved the way, and, most importantly, ensures we keep moving forward, learning from both our triumphs and our missteps. While dwelling on the past can hold us back, understanding it can propel us onward.

When I first entered this field in 1984, Miami Vice was debuting on television, the Apple Macintosh had just hit the market, and the Dow Jones was hovering around 1,100 points. In our field, we were sheltering 14 to 15 million dogs and cats every year. Few shelters had veterinarians on staff, and shelter medicine as a specialty didn't exist. Most animal shelters were bare-bones facilities, often placed near landfills or wastewater treatment plants. There was tension between nonprofit organizations and municipal animal control agencies, and even more friction between the veterinary community and those working to save shelter pets. Formal training was scarce. Most of us learned on the job, doing the best we could with what we had.

Fast forward to today. We stream content on demand, our phones double as mini supercomputers, and the Dow has surpassed 40,000 points. And in animal welfare? The progress has been just as remarkable. According to *Shelter Animals Count*, approximately 6.5

million animals now pass through the shelter system each year—a decrease of more than 50% from 40 years ago. Few social movements have seen such dramatic, measurable success in such a short time. The animal welfare workforce is more highly trained than ever before, with certification programs, advanced shelter medicine specialties, and leadership training now readily available. The field has evolved from a grassroots effort into a professional, data-driven industry focused on sustainable solutions.

And yet, some of the most persistent challenges from the early years remain. Infighting among organizations and individuals has been a constant struggle, and social media has only amplified the divisions. Early in my career, I watched as staff, board members, and volunteers left established organizations to start competing groups—not to expand services, but often in opposition to one another. I've seen talented people spend more energy attacking others in the field than helping animals.

Decades later, this pattern continues, and the damage it causes is profound. The blame game distracts from the mission, misleads the public, and weakens the very organizations working toward lifesaving solutions. Still, when tensions run high, I remind myself that much of this comes from a place of passion—from people who care deeply. We may not always agree on how to get there, but we are, in the end, working toward the same goal: *to help animals and the people who care for them*.

That's why it's so important to reframe the narrative—to shift the focus from blame to shared responsibility.

To paraphrase a wise leader in our field, *"Blaming shelters for euthanasia is like blaming the American Cancer Society for cancer."*[1] The people working in this space—whether in shelters, rescues, advocacy, or veterinary care—are here because they care. No one group or philosophy has a monopoly on compassion. The

1 Tedford attributes this quote to Pam Burns, former President and CEO of the Hawaiian Humane Society, who served in the role for 27 years. A nationally respected voice in animal welfare, she was known for her ability to bring people together across differing viewpoints. Pam championed humane education, legislative advocacy, and community engagement throughout Hawai'i and beyond. Her legacy continues to inspire leaders across the field.

real challenge is not deciding who cares more, but how we work together to make that caring count.

Which brings me to this book.

Humane Perspectives is a celebration of what's possible when people lead with both heart and humility. The leaders featured here didn't write their stories to seek praise; they wrote them to pass the baton. To say: *"Here's what I've learned. These are my experiences. Maybe they'll help you, too."*

These are people who have shaped the field from the ground up. Some began as volunteers, others in the kennels, gradually working their way into leadership roles. Still others came from the corporate world, the arts, legal fields, or the front lines of public service. They didn't follow the same path, but each of them has paved the way for others. They've changed systems, built programs, stabilized organizations, and created cultures where both people and animals can thrive. Their wisdom is hard-won. Their honesty is refreshing. And their stories are filled with lessons you won't find in a textbook or a leadership course—lessons earned through trial, reflection, and perseverance.

What unites them isn't where they came from. It's how they show up—with empathy, with vision, and with the willingness to do the hard work of leading in a field that doesn't always make it easy.

The future of animal welfare is bright. Talented, passionate leaders are emerging every day, ready to carry the mission forward. And while 40 years may feel like a long time for those of us who've lived through this transformation, in the grand scheme of things, it's just the beginning of what's possible.

This book isn't just about where we've been, it's about where we're going. It's about leadership, vision, and the collective power we have to shape the future of animal welfare together. As you read the stories and insights from some of our field's most thoughtful voices, I hope you'll be reminded of what unites us, rather than what divides us.

The next chapter of this movement will be written by those who step up, collaborate, and lead with integrity. May these stories inspire you to lead with compassion, break down barriers, and work together to build a future where every animal—and every community—receives the care and support they deserve.

To the contributors of this book: thank you. Your leadership is a powerful reminder that this movement is built by those who keep showing up, who ask the hard questions, and who refuse to settle for "*good enough*." You are the ones pushing for a future that's more humane, more just, and more compassionate—for animals and the people who care for them.

A special thank you to **Cathy M. Rosenthal** for bringing these voices together. I've known Cathy for a long time, and while she doesn't seek the spotlight, she has been a steady force behind the scenes, shaping conversations and elevating ideas through her writing and training programs for people in the animal welfare field for more than 35 years. She'll tell you herself: her passion isn't managing teams or running shelters but telling stories that lift others up. Her vision, persistence, and deep commitment to amplifying leadership across the animal welfare field made this book possible.

If you're stepping into leadership now, I hope this book gives you courage. If you've been doing this work a long time, I hope it reminds you that you're not alone. And if you're wondering whether your voice matters—*let me assure you, it does.*

May this book be your companion, your spark, and your reminder that the future of animal welfare isn't just possible, it's being built every day.

One story, one leader, one lesson at a time.

***Jim Tedford** joined The Association for Animal Welfare Advancement (formerly SAWA) as President & CEO in June 2015—a role he embraced as his "dream job." But his connection to the organization runs much deeper. He has been a member for nearly 30 years and served as board chair more than 20 years ago.*

With over 40 years of experience in the animal welfare field, Tedford has led sheltering organizations in New York, Louisiana, and Tennessee, and served as a regional director for The Humane Society of the United States (currently known as Humane World for Animals). Early in his career, he worked in what he fondly calls, "tiny humane societies held together with duct tape and love." He later applied his nonprofit expertise in direct-response marketing to support shelters and advocacy groups nationwide.

A sought-after speaker, Tedford frequently gives presentations on leadership, organizational strategy, data-driven practices, and shelter medicine. He holds a bachelor's degree in animal science from the University of Tennessee-Knoxville, and is a Certified Animal Welfare Administrator (CAWA)[2]*.*

Tedford and his wife, Ann, share their home with three energetic terriers, a rescued macaw, and Handsome Sam, an off-the-track thoroughbred. They love the outdoors and often retreat to nature with their travel trailer—a peaceful contrast to the urgency of animal welfare, and a reminder of the deeper connections they work to protect every day.

2 CAWA is a professional credential recognizing advanced knowledge and leadership in the animal welfare field, awarded by the Association for Animal Welfare Advancement (AAWA).

"The future of our field depends on reimagining our business models, so that they value people as much as programs."

2

Raissa Allaire

Listening Before Leading: Lessons from a Winding Road

If you look at my résumé, you would see a winding path rather than a straight line. I began my career in the for-profit sector with a degree in English from the University of Chicago, a master's degree with an emphasis on cultural policy, and experience in public relations. I launched and managed national campaigns for healthcare organizations, museums, and nonprofits—projects that honed my ability to craft compelling messages and mobilize support for a cause.

Somewhere in that work, I discovered the allure of the nonprofit world: the sense of mission, the conviction that every effort is tied to improving people's lives. That pull led me deeper into museum work, where my curiosity pushed me to learn every aspect of the field—from archives and education to collections, development, and strategic planning. Eventually, I transitioned into social services, serving first as a marketing and development director and then as the Chief Operating Officer of a mid-size organization supporting 20,000 Illinois families annually. There, I learned how policy, advocacy, and direct service intersect to create systemic change, and I began to see leadership as an opportunity to bridge big-picture strategy with the day-to-day realities of frontline work.

And then, unexpectedly, animal welfare found me. My family adopted two orange tabbies—our first pets—and they changed us forever. Those cats opened a new part of my heart and my worldview. I saw how deeply animals can transform human lives and how they can be anchors of love and stability. I became curious about the systems that protected and advocated for them.

So, when the executive director position at Tree House Humane Society opened in 2018, I didn't have a background in sheltering beyond my cats. But I recognized the opportunity to lead an organization with a strong legacy and untapped potential for greater impact. My experiences in communication, strategy, and organizational turnaround had prepared me for complex challenges. What I didn't yet know about animal welfare, I could learn. And in many ways, that willingness to learn became my most important leadership tool in the years ahead.

Stepping into Crisis

When I stepped into the role of Executive Director, Tree House was at a pivotal moment of change. The organization had recently transitioned from a grassroots rescue operating out of a house into a $7 million, state-of-the-art shelter. Alongside that move came a major rebrand and, most notably, the decision to remove "no-kill" from our mission statement, as I felt it had become a divisive term in the field. A difficult behavioral euthanasia decision further heightened tensions, leaving some longtime supporters feeling alienated. Staff and volunteers were voicing concerns publicly, donors were questioning their support, and the weight of a new mortgage loomed over the organization, adding financial strain to an already turbulent time.

I knew my first priority wasn't to make changes—it was to understand the depth and nuance of the rift. So, I went on a listening tour. I met one-on-one and in small groups with staff, board members, former volunteers, donors, and even some of our most outspoken critics. I asked trusted advisors for introductions to people who believed Tree House had lost its way, and I sought them out.

These conversations weren't about defending the past or convincing anyone of my point of view. My role was to listen without interruption, acknowledge their experiences, and make sure they knew they had been heard. I took notes, asked follow-up questions, and later provided clear, transparent information—explaining how euthanasia decisions are made, sharing how the board was committed and evolving, and outlining the commitments that would guide us moving forward. Over time, these open conversations began to rebuild trust and lay the groundwork for real change.

From Warrior Mode to Diplomacy

Early in my career, I equated leadership with always holding firm, charging ahead, and "being right." That mindset served me well in moments of crisis, but I learned that sustained leadership requires a different skill set—one grounded in self-awareness, adaptability, and the ability to bring people with you rather than simply pushing them forward.

I began to see that my role was not to win every battle, but to know my guardrails—those non-negotiable values and priorities—while meeting people where they were. True influence came from demonstrating, through consistent actions more than declarations, that trust could be rebuilt. This required regulating my own urgency, recognizing that while some changes must happen quickly to stabilize an organization, others require patience, persistence, and an acceptance of incremental progress.

I also invested in building resilience for the long journey ahead. I developed a personal "cabinet" of advisors—respected leaders from inside and outside the animal welfare field—who could offer unvarnished feedback and diverse perspectives. They challenged my assumptions, helped me think strategically about financial turnaround (we faced $2.5 million in debt when I arrived), guided me in strengthening the board, and encouraged me to approach cultural change with both vision and diplomacy.

Their honesty was often uncomfortable but always invaluable. It pushed me to grow as a leader—not just in skill, but in emotional intelligence, humility, and the ability to navigate complexity. One of the best pieces of advice I've ever received was this: *"You can be right, but you don't always have to be right in the moment."* I came to see it as an invitation to lead differently—to pause, listen, and allow understanding to come before solutions. As a result, I try to offer the same kind of candid, constructive support to other leaders who find themselves walking the same tightrope between urgency and patience, resolve and openness.

Building for the Future

Today, Tree House is debt-free, with a $5 million budget, a thriving low-cost wellness center, and a board culture rooted in trust, accountability, and collaboration. What I value most is the mutual accountability we've built. My leadership team and I push one another to be better, stand together when it matters most, and stay deeply aligned in our commitment to a mission that feels stronger and more united than ever.

Looking back, one of my biggest lessons is the importance of investing early in the well-being of the people who make the mission possible. If I could start over as an executive director, I would have moved faster on staff wage increases, benefits, and wellness initiatives. Animal welfare—like much of the nonprofit sector—has long been trapped in the "starvation cycle," where public and donor skepticism about paying competitive salaries forces organizations to do more with less, often at the expense of the very people doing the work.

This mindset comes at a high cost: chronic understaffing, burnout, and high turnover. I've learned that sustainability is not just about balancing a budget—it's about building a workplace that retains and inspires talented people over the long term. That means challenging outdated assumptions, advocating for fair pay and realistic workloads, and communicating transparently with donors about why investing in staff is one of the most direct ways to improve animal welfare outcomes.

The future of our field depends on reimagining our business models so that they value people as much as programs. We must be willing to innovate, diversify our revenue streams, and tell a new story—one that shows donors and the public that when we take care of our people, they can take even better care of the animals.

Never Stop Learning

One of my earliest mentors was a senior intern from my social services days—a man decades older than me who approached new technology with the curiosity of a student. He never let pride or comfort stand in the way of growth. That openness shaped my philosophy: stay curious, keep learning, and never assume you've "arrived" as a leader.

Even now, I push myself into new learning curves. I'm currently enrolled in a course on AI and business transformation. It's both exciting and a little daunting, which is exactly the right combination for growth. The world is changing, the needs of our communities are changing, so the way we serve animals must evolve, too.

But I've learned that the single most powerful tool a leader can possess is the ability to listen. Listening without an agenda can turn conflict into connection, suspicion into trust, and crisis into a foundation for lasting change. It's not easy, and sometimes you will have missteps, but you just keep getting up.

At Tree House, listening turned protest lines into partnerships, angry letters into productive dialogue, and uncertainty into a shared vision for the future. It's what allowed us to transition from a place of crisis to one of strength.

And here's the thing: you don't have to lead an organization to effect change. Whether you manage a team, volunteer at a shelter, or simply want to make a difference in your community, the same principles apply. Stay curious. Be willing to adapt. And listen deeply enough to transform moments into turning points. That's where trust is built, where possibilities open up, and where real change begins.

Raissa Allaire has served as Executive Director of Tree House Humane Society in Chicago, Illinois, since 2018, bringing more than 20 years of nonprofit leadership experience spanning social services, arts, and animal welfare. Under her guidance, Tree House has expanded its reach and resilience—launching the Tree House Veterinary Wellness

Center, quadrupling financial reserves, eliminating organizational debt, and leading a bold rebrand to strengthen its connection with mission and community.

Allaire's path to animal welfare was sparked by adopting her family's first pets, which inspired her to bring her skills in strategy, operations, and mission-driven storytelling into the service of animals. Prior to joining Tree House, she served as Chief Operating Officer of a mid-sized social services organization, overseeing programs that annually served 20,000 Illinois families, and as Vice President/Chief of Staff at a Chicago-based museum.

Allaire is a recognized leader in organizational transformation, board development, and building cultures of trust and innovation. She has been selected for prestigious leadership initiatives, including the Allstate-Kellogg Greater Good Nonprofit Leadership Program and Bridgespan's Leading for Impact. She is currently the Board Chair of The Association for Animal Welfare Advancement and previously co-chaired the Chicagoland Humane Coalition.

A lifelong learner, Allaire holds undergraduate and graduate degrees from the University of Chicago and is currently exploring how AI and emerging technologies can elevate social impact work. At home, she shares her life with her family and two orange tabbies, and finds joy in gardening, reading Harvard Business Review articles, and championing sustainability and well-being for those who care for animals.

*"Love is what brings you here,
resilience is what keeps you here."*

3

Shafonda Davis Allen

What I Wish I Knew Before Starting in this Field

I have worked in animal welfare for 27 years.

I started as an adoption counselor with a fierce love of animals, and over time—through education and commitment—I worked my way up, learning as I went along. I eventually became the Shelter Director in 2008 and the Executive Director in 2014 for the Animal Protection Society of Durham in Durham, North Carolina. I have served on state and national boards and am an esteemed national welfare leader, holding a CAWA (Certified Animal Welfare Administrator) designation. I am also among the top 1% of BIPOC (Black, Indigenous, and People of Color) leaders in my position in the United States.

By all accounts, I may be considered a trailblazer, but to me, this work is simply who I am. Once I stepped into the world of animal welfare, there was no walking away. What began as simple visits to the shelter with my two small children quickly turned into something more when, after a few weeks of stopping by to see the animals, I asked if they were hiring—and they were. I started the very next week and never looked back. It was as if I had found my people, my purpose, and my life. I belonged here.

And, here is what I have learned along the way.

Learning to Last in Animal Welfare. Why Passion isn't Enough.

When I started in animal welfare, it was my love for animals that brought me through the shelter doors. And, I thought that passion alone would be enough to sustain me. I quickly learned that while love is what brings you here, resilience is what keeps you here. This work is so much more than a job; it's a lifestyle. For some, the pace and the emotional demands can make it unsustainable. For others, like me, it becomes truly addictive and all-consuming.

→ *You have to find ways to adapt, pace yourself, and protect your energy so you can continue to show up for the animals and the people who rely on you.*

The Higher You Climb, the More You See

I began as an adoption counselor with a heart for each animal I met. Over time, I worked my way up—first to an adoption manager, then to a shelter director, and ultimately to an executive director. With each step, my perspective widened. Initially, I focused on individual animals and their unique personalities. As I moved into higher leadership roles, I began to see them as part of a much bigger picture—a tide of lives that needed to be managed in a way that kept the entire environment safe and secure.

→ *Leadership means caring deeply for each life, while taking responsibility for the bigger picture.*

Remember to Breathe

Effective leadership in animal welfare requires more than just caring for animals. It requires diplomacy, grit, and the ability to keep going day after day. It's not just about feeding or promoting an animal. It's about sustaining an entire organization for the good of all: the animals, the people, and the community. There are days when the demands can consume you, leaving little room for a sense of self. Sometimes, you don't even give yourself permission to stop and breathe.

→ *Make yourself pause now and then. Take a breath. You'll need it to last in this work.*

Learn to Lead with Heart—and Strategy

If you're entering this field, understand that leadership here is not driven by heart alone. The heart is what connects you to the mission. It's what makes you fight for every animal and every person you serve. But strategy is what turns that passion into real, lasting change. Strong leadership means knowing how to plan, manage resources, and make difficult decisions that strike a balance between compassion and practicality.

→ *The heart keeps you showing up; the strategy ensures your work leaves a sustainable legacy. Without both, even the most dedicated leader will burn out before their vision is realized.*

Find Joy Between the Heartbreak

What I wish I had known at the start is that this job isn't easy. You will experience loss, frustration, grief, and moments that break your heart. But you will also experience joy—pure, undeniable joy—that makes it all worth it. Those moments of joy will remind you why you started in this work in the first place—and why, despite the challenges, you stay. They are the reason I still walk into the shelter each day ready to do this work.

→ *Hold on fiercely to those joyful moments. They are what will carry you through difficult times.*

Shafonda Davis Allen *has dedicated over two decades to promoting the well-being of animals and the communities that care for them. For more than 12 years, she served as Executive Director of the Animal Protection Society of Durham, guiding the organization through growth and challenges with an unwavering focus on lifesaving outcomes.*

Shafonda began her career as an adoption counselor, driven by a deep love for animals. Through dedication, on-the-job learning, and continued education, she advanced into leadership roles - first as Shelter Director and ultimately as Executive Director. Along the way, she earned her Certified Animal Welfare Administrator (CAWA) designation and became a respected voice in the field of animal welfare.

Today, she serves on the board of the Association for Animal Welfare Advancement and is a member of its Diversity, Equity, and Inclusion (DEI) Council, where she contributes her voice and perspective as one of the few BIPOC leaders in the animal welfare field. She previously served on the boards of the North Carolina Animal Federation as well as Companions and Animals for Reform and Equity.

Her leadership blends compassion with strategic vision. She is a strong advocate for community partnerships, volunteer engagement, and inclusive practices, believing that shelters thrive when they are deeply connected to the people they serve. In her own words, animal welfare is more than a career - it's a lifestyle that demands resilience and the ability to find joy even in the most challenging moments.

A proud Durham native, Shafonda was educated in Durham County Public Schools and attended Durham Technical Community College. She credits her professional knowledge to years of hands-on experience and field-specific educational opportunities.

Outside of work, she shares her life with her husband, two senior pets, four children, and three grandchildren, who bring her immense joy. And, as she likes to say, "Tell no one, but I love kids as much as I love animals."

*"You can do your job without me,
but I can't do mine without you."*

4

Mike Arms

Compassion Meets Business Savvy

What does it take to be a leader in animal welfare?

It's not just about loving animals—though that's essential—it's about blending compassion with strategy, heart with purpose, and learning how to make real, lasting change for both animals and the people who care for them.

My journey has been filled with lessons, challenges, and triumphs, and each experience has shaped my approach to leadership. If you're stepping into this field with a desire to lead, I hope the following insights and reflections will inspire you as you embark on your own path.

Early Lessons

One of the most formative moments in my career was early on, when I worked at the American Society for the Prevention of Cruelty to Animals (ASPCA) in New York City. Surrounded by like-minded individuals who cared deeply for animals, I was inspired by the power of compassion. Later, my time at North Shore Animal League in Port Washington, New York, allowed me to work with remarkable mentors like Alex Lewyt, who helped me see that to truly succeed in animal welfare, we must apply sound business principles without losing our hearts. Alex taught me that success in animal welfare requires more than passion—it requires a strategic approach rooted in sound business principles. His guidance taught me to "run the business with a heart," which became the foundation of my leadership philosophy.

It's easy to get swept up in the emotional side of animal welfare, but as Alex taught me, a leader must strike a balance between passion and practicality. That message has stayed with me my entire career, and I believe it's foundational for anyone who wants to make a lasting impact in this field.

The Power of Mission-Driven Leadership

In animal welfare, our work is about more than just helping animals—it's about building a movement. One of the most rewarding parts of my journey has been creating programs that connect people and organizations globally. Initiatives like *Home 4 the Holidays* and *Remember Me Thursday* have brought together hundreds of groups worldwide to raise awareness and find homes for orphaned pets. Staying focused on this broader mission, rather than getting bogged down by everyday challenges, has allowed us to reach more animals and involve more communities in our cause.

For leaders, having a clear mission is essential, but it's equally important to keep that mission front and center for your team. At Helen Woodward Animal Center in Rancho Santa Fe, California, we gather for an all-staff meeting each month, where I share our latest successes and personally thank the team for their efforts. Celebrating wins together, however big or small, keeps us all connected to our purpose and reminds us of the difference we're making in the lives of animals and families. I encourage aspiring leaders to foster that same spirit of gratitude and unity within their teams.

Overcoming Challenges with Resilience

Animal welfare can be emotionally demanding, and burnout is a real risk, especially for leaders who feel responsible for their staff and the animals. One of the best pieces of advice I can offer is to stay focused on the positive impact you're creating. In nearly 60 years of work, I've faced my share of challenges, but I keep my motivation alive by remembering the millions of lives we've saved, rather than dwelling on daily struggles.

Early on, I learned the importance of resilience. When I first began introducing business and marketing practices to animal shelters, I faced a lot of resistance. People worried these strategies were too "corporate" for a compassionate field. But over time, as they saw how these changes increased adoptions and reduced euthanasia, they understood. Staying true to my vision, even in the face of skepticism, taught me that with patience and perseverance, we can inspire others to see new possibilities.

One of the biggest challenges was shifting perspectives about shelter operations. I remember the looks on my staff's faces when I explained they needed to control their inventory rather than let their inventory control them. Comments like, *"These aren't inventory, these are live pets,"* were common. I asked them to explain the difference, and when they couldn't, it opened the door for deeper conversations. It took time, but once they embraced this mindset, it improved outcomes for the animals in their care.

Fostering a Positive and Collaborative Environment

Leadership isn't just about having a vision. It's about building a positive and collaborative environment where everyone feels valued. I've learned that recognition and gratitude go a long way in keeping a team motivated. Every month, we provide lunch for the entire team and celebrate each department's accomplishments, reminding everyone how their work fits into the larger mission. Little gestures like this build camaraderie and reinforce the sense of family that so many in animal welfare cherish.

When COVID-19 hit, we faced unique challenges. Many of our employees were struggling to balance work and childcare as schools moved to remote learning. To support them, we set up an area at the Center with desks, dividers, and credentialed teachers, allowing parents to bring their children to work. This gesture wasn't just about logistics—it showed our team that we're a community that cares for one another. I truly believe that leadership is about showing up for your people, and when you do, they show up for the animals with renewed dedication.

Encouraging Growth and Mentorship

Mentorship is at the heart of effective leadership. When I joined the Helen Woodward Animal Center in 1999, I realized the importance of operating with the discipline and strategy of a business, even as a nonprofit organization. To help our team understand this, I sent our adoptions staff to local retail stores, asking them to observe customer service and branding practices. It was a hands-on lesson in the power of professionalism and marketing in promoting adoptions.

Mentoring isn't just about giving advice; it's about opening doors for others and sharing the lessons that shaped you. With *The Business of Saving Lives* workshops, we provide training in marketing, fundraising, and social media strategies to animal welfare groups around the world. We travel to them, sometimes at our own expense, because I believe in paying it forward. If I can help another organization succeed, then we all win. I encourage future leaders to mentor with that same sense of generosity—it not only strengthens your team but also multiplies your impact across the field.

Staying Mission-Driven for Success

Success in leadership often comes with recognition, but it's important to stay humble and focused on the mission rather than personal accolades. I regularly remind our team that they are the backbone of our success. I tell our volunteers and staff, *"You can do your job without me, but I can't do mine without you."* Recognizing others' efforts helps build trust and respect, ensuring that each person feels valued and appreciated.

One of the toughest lessons I learned early on was that success in this field doesn't happen in isolation. A perfect example of this was the creation of two programs that initially met with some resistance from staff. The first event was *Remember Me Thursday®* in 2012. This event unites individuals and pet adoption organizations worldwide as a unified voice for orphan pets in need of forever homes, honoring those who didn't make it and shining a light on those still waiting. The other program was *Surf Dog Surf-a-Thon*, launched in 2005, a surfing competition and fundraiser featuring dogs of all sizes and breeds riding the waves. (It is now the longest-running canine surf competition in the United States.)

When I first proposed these ideas to two managers—one in social media and the other in information technology—I was met with doubt. Both said they didn't think it could be done. Rather than letting their skepticism derail the idea, I asked them to meet with me and bring a list of obstacles they saw in the way. Together, we went through each challenge, finding solutions step by step. By working collaboratively, we turned hesitation into action and made it happen. Today, *Remember Me Thursday* is an annual global event, and *Surf Dog* draws attention from around the world.

These experiences reinforced for me that success is built on collective action, shared passion, and teamwork. Leaders who listen, share credit, and celebrate their teams' contributions cultivate a positive, sustainable culture that fuels long-term success.

Balancing Heart and Practicality

In animal welfare, leaders must balance compassion with practicality. We all come to this field with a deep love for animals, but to make an impact, we need to think strategically. Early on, I realized that passion alone wasn't enough. Leaders in animal welfare need to approach their work with the same principles as any successful organization: clear goals, effective marketing, and sound management. This doesn't diminish our compassion; rather, it allows us to channel it into tangible results.

For those new to leadership, remember that it's okay to make mistakes, as long as you're willing to learn from them. Be open to feedback, take responsibility for your actions, and always keep the mission at the forefront. It's easy to get bogged down by challenges, but staying focused on the positive impact you can make is what sustains you through the ups and downs.

Leaving a Legacy

As leaders, we hope to leave a lasting impact that will carry on beyond our time. Programs like *Home 4 the Holidays* and *Remember Me Thursday* were created to inspire global action for orphan pets, and I hope these initiatives continue long into the future. Watching other organizations adopt similar models has shown me that when we share our ideas freely, we inspire a ripple effect that multiplies our impact.

Leadership in animal welfare is not just about saving lives—it's about building a compassionate movement. Each of us has the power to inspire others, whether through mentorship, collaboration, or simply by showing up with heart and purpose. If you're starting your journey, remember that your work can create meaningful change. Embrace your passion, learn continuously, and never underestimate the impact of bringing people together to work toward a common goal.

Each of us has a role to play, and every small action contributes to a larger, more compassionate world. Together, through leadership rooted in love and resilience, we can make a lasting difference for animals and the people who care for them.

***Mike Arms** is a pioneer in animal welfare whose vision and determination have saved the lives of millions of orphaned pets. He's the creative force behind the International Pet Adopt-a-thon, Home 4 the Holidays, Remember Me Thursday, and Surf Dog Surf-a-Thon—campaigns that have inspired shelters and adopters around the globe.*

His life's mission began in the late 1960s while working for the American Society for the Prevention of Cruelty to Animals (ASPCA). Answering a call about an injured dog, Arms found not only a badly hurt puppy but also cruelty so shocking it changed him forever. As he bent to rescue the dog, he was attacked by onlookers who had been betting on how long the dog would survive. The dog, unable to walk, crawled to his side and licked him back to consciousness. Arms made a promise to God that day: if he lived, he would spend his life protecting animals. He's kept that promise ever since.

After 20 years at North Shore Animal League, Arms became President of the Helen Woodward Animal Center in Rancho Santa Fe, California, in 1999. Under his leadership, pet adoptions tripled, humane education now reaches over 15,000 children annually, and his

Business of Saving Lives workshops, created by Arms and taught by the Center's team leaders, have helped more than 600 organizations in 40 states and 20 countries learn how to find families for orphaned pets, raise the funds to support their work, and use public relations and social media to build their brand. Arms is also a sought-after speaker, sharing his expertise at conferences, corporate events, and as a keynote presenter worldwide.

Arms' work connects people and animals in extraordinary ways. His leadership blends creativity, compassion, and a fierce belief that when we work together, we can change the world for pets.

"The love people have for our best friends on four legs is a godsend. It's what fuels our work, our mission, and our movement. We are fortunate to be part of a cause that not only fulfills what's in our hearts but also reflects a shared desire—across our communities, our states, and our country—to create a more compassionate world for animals."

Richard Avanzino

What Saving One Dog Taught Me About Changing the World

I never imagined that a headhunter's call would change the course of my life—or help change the course of animal welfare in America.

In 1976, I was working in Southern California as an administrator for the Orange County Health Planning Council. I had degrees in pharmacy and law, worked as a lobbyist, and had drafted healthcare legislation for the California Legislature. I had no background in animal welfare, but loved animals. So, when a recruiter called me and described an opportunity at the San Francisco SPCA (SF SPCA), something clicked. I had always loved animals and had once hoped to become a veterinarian, but I couldn't handle the dissection work required in veterinary school, so I changed direction. Here, finally, was a chance to serve animals in a different way. I took the job, not knowing that it would become a lifelong calling.

When I arrived at the SF SPCA, the organization was on the brink of bankruptcy. During the interview process, the board asked what I would do to turn things around. I told them, *"There are three steps: 1) Do a good job; 2) Tell people about it; then, 3) Ask for help."* That philosophy not only saved the organization, it also helped us become one of the wealthiest and most innovative shelter operations in the country

But our greatest success wasn't financial. It was moral. And it began with a little dog named Sido.

The Sido Story

Sido was an 11-year-old Sheltie-mix whose owner had passed away and left a heartbreaking request in her will: that Sido be euthanized. The owner feared her beloved dog might be placed in a home that didn't love her—or she would end up in animal experimentation, which was not possible in San Francisco but was happening elsewhere in the country. At that time, the SF SPCA was also the city's animal control agency, caring for abandoned animals like Sido. So, when we received the directive from the executor of the will to euthanize Sido, I politely said, *"No."*

Our belief was that every animal deserves a chance to find a home, and we were willing to stake everything on it. But the executor warned us: if we didn't comply with the will's directive as required by law, we would be sued, the SPCA would be bankrupted, and we would lose everything. I stood firm. I took Sido home that night, introduced her to my family, and told them, *"She'll be living with us while we fight this."*

Sido became a fixture in our lives—a loyal, loving companion, never more than a few feet away from me. She followed me through the shelter, slept by my side at home, and even grew jealous when my wife came to bed, letting out a low growl before allowing her to lie down. We bonded deeply. And, for six months, we fought for her life. We brought on attorneys, reached out to the Animal Legal Defense Fund, and pleaded with lawmakers.

Eventually, the story broke through to the city. I had invited a local reporter to meet Sido. Sido walked up to the reporter, rested her body on his leg, and gently licked his hand as he was about to write about her. The reporter immediately said, *"I get it,"* acknowledging why we're fighting so hard. The story exploded in the media—radio, TV, and print. Everyone wanted to know about this little dog whose life hung in the balance. A state senator even introduced legislation to protect her. Both houses passed it in 45 days, despite objections from well-known national animal groups.

But 40 days passed, and the governor hadn't signed the bill. We were due in court the next day. I feared the worst. I told my wife that if the court didn't rule in our favor, I was prepared to go to jail to protect Sido. I sequestered Sido in a safe house with a coworker to guard her because if the decision went against us, I had no intention of handing her over. We were not going to let her die. Period.

On the day of the trial, the courtroom was packed with supporters. TV crews filled the aisles. I was tense, bracing for whatever might come next. Then, halfway through the hearing, the courtroom phone rang. The clerk picked it up and handed it to the judge, saying quietly, *"The governor is on the line."* The room went silent. We watched as the judge listened and nodded. Finally, he hung up, looked out at the courtroom, and said, *"That was Governor Brown. He has decided to sign the legislation."*

He paused, and said, *"But he's too late. I'm going to rule on this case."*

What!? My heart sank. There was a hush across the courtroom as we all waited for what we feared was the worst.

"I'm ruling that animals have rights," he said. *"If there is a loving home available, they cannot be killed."*

I was stunned! The courtroom erupted in emotion.

I called Sido's temporary caregiver to bring Sido to the courthouse. I was waiting on the courthouse steps when she arrived. As she walked toward all the people gathered on the steps, Sido spotted me from across the street. She broke loose of her leash and darted across a busy San Francisco street. My heart stopped. I was terrified she would be hit by a car. A police officer, seeing what was happening, stepped in front of the cars and stopped the traffic. She ran straight into my arms and leapt up to kiss me. The cameras were rolling. It was a moment I will never forget.

That moment became the start of the no-kill movement for me. Because what I learned through Sido was this: if you tell an animal's story, people will care. The community will rally. Americans love animals deeply, and they will act.

Telling Our Stories to the Community

Even before Sido's case, I encouraged staff to share what they saw and experienced in the shelter and out in the field. I wanted the public to see what I saw—that the work we did every day was extraordinary. But when I asked staff, *"What's new? What's going on?"* they would say, *"Just the usual."* Until one veterinary technician said, *"I don't have time, Rich—we're doing surgery on a dog that fell from a fourth-story window, and we just found a gold coin in her stomach."*

I stood there, amazed. I thought, *"This is what you do every day? Dogs falling from windows and gold coins in their stomachs—and you think that's nothing worth mentioning?"* I realized we were missing an incredible opportunity to share these moments with the world.

Storytelling became central to our mission. So, I made a rule: every department submitted one story a week, and every employee submitted one every six months. Nothing had to be polished—it just had to be real.

One day, I asked one of our veterinarians to appear on television to discuss a cat that had been set on fire. He was the one treating the cat, after all, and would be the best person to tell his story.

He refused at first. *"I'm a surgeon, not a PR guy,"* he said.

But I arranged for him to meet with the news crew anyway. When he told the story, it came from someone who had directly cared for that cat—not secondhand through me. The next day, his friends and neighbors called to say how proud they were of him. A week later, the doctor came to me and said, *"Hey, can I do that again?"*

That was the magic. By the time I left, 145 people in our organization were sharing stories, and we were asking the community for help in myriad ways. The people of San Francisco always responded.

The Birth of Maddie's Fund®

After 23 years at the SF SPCA, I joined Dave and Cheryl Duffield to establish Maddie's Fund, a family foundation named after their beloved dog, Maddie. Their $300 million gift wasn't just about generosity; it was about transforming the entire field of animal welfare. They believed we could build a no-kill nation. And so did I.

The vision was bold: to fund communities, not just individual shelters, with an infusion of much-needed resources over a five-year period, accompanied by a plan for achieving quantifiable results and sustainability. This would require collaboration between large and small organizations, the collection and sharing of statistics, and an end to infighting. We made it clear—no more bashing and trashing each other. If you wanted funding, you had to work together, respect each other, and be transparent.

We referred to it as "performance-based philanthropy." We paid for results—measurable outcomes, not promises. We insisted on data collection long before It was standard. And we supported communities who were ready to take bold steps together.

Dave was criticized in the press for doing this. One article in the Wall Street Journal questioned why he would give so much to animals when there were "more important causes" out there. But Dave didn't flinch. He believed companion animals were worthy of our deepest commitment—and he inspired a new wave of donors who shared his sentiment.

Dave and Cheryl's generosity helped elevate animal welfare as a cause worthy of serious philanthropic investment—and proved that outcomes, not just intentions, can drive real change.

Advice for Young Leaders

The animal welfare field can feel overwhelming at times, but it's also one of the most meaningful places to invest your time, energy, and heart. Whether you're starting as a volunteer, a staff member, or stepping into leadership, here's what I have learned:

1. **Take risks.** Don't be afraid to go against the grain if it's the right thing to do for animals. You might be alone at first, but leadership means stepping forward when it counts.

2. Speak from your heart. People don't connect with policies—they connect with passion. Be honest. Be human. Let people see what this work means to *you*.

3. Tell people what you're doing. Don't assume people know the difference you're making. Show them. Share the stories. Ask for help. You'll be surprised by how many will say yes.

4. Surround yourself with people who care. Hire for heart. When I interviewed candidates, I didn't care much about their resumes. I cared about how they interacted with others and how much love they brought to the mission. That's the secret sauce.

5. Know that leadership isn't about titles. It's about being present and listening to others. It's about being willing to go to jail for what's right, if it comes to that. And it's about giving others a reason to believe that we can do better—together.

I've seen a lot in this world—some of it heartbreaking. The news can feel heavy with tragedy, cruelty, and injustice. But when I think about what we're doing for our best friends on four legs, I'm reminded of the beauty and purpose in this work. It offers hope, a pause from the weight of the world. It brings joy, meaning, and connection.

I'll never forget Sido. Or the staff who told stories and, in doing so, helped raise millions. Or the public who opened their hearts to so many animals in need.

Behind every animal saved is a person—often many—who made that outcome possible. A staff member, an adopter, a volunteer, a donor—each one turning compassion into action. It's the people with the passion to help animals, and the willingness to show up every day, who make the difference.

We are lucky—so lucky—to do this work. And I believe, with passion, persistence, and a shared purpose, we truly can save them all.

***Richard Avanzino**, widely recognized as the father of the no-kill movement, spent nearly four decades transforming animal welfare with bold ideas, visionary leadership, and unwavering compassion. His core belief—that all shelter pets deserve a loving home—redefined* *the role of shelters across America and helped elevate companion animals from property to family.*

Avanzino served as President of the SF SPCA from 1976 to 1999, rescuing the organization from financial ruin and pioneering a host of lifesaving innovations. He famously led the legal and legislative charge to save Sido, an elderly pet condemned in a will—a case that changed California law and redefined society's view of animals as sentient beings, not property.

Under his leadership, San Francisco became the first major city in the U.S. to guarantee adoption for every healthy and treatable shelter pet. His groundbreaking programs in adoption, foster care, spay/neuter, and animal behavior became models for shelters nationwide. In 1998, he opened the Maddie's® Pet Adoption Center, revolutionizing animal sheltering by replacing cages with cozy, home-like adoption suites—a standard now widely emulated.

In 1999, Avanzino joined Maddie's Fund as its President, where he directed the foundation's $300 million endowment to drive transformative change in U.S. shelters. He launched key initiatives including shelter medicine programs at top veterinary schools, high-volume adoption events, data-driven accountability systems, and grant programs that empowered local and national organizations to adopt the no-kill vision.

Avanzino's influence extends well beyond institutional leadership. He is known for innovative programs like mobile spay/neuter clinics, community foster networks, humane volunteer programs, and media-savvy promotions (like "Bucks for Balls") that helped engage communities in lifesaving work.

Avanzino holds a Doctor of Pharmacy degree and a law degree from the University of California and remains a sought-after strategic advisor in animal welfare. Though retired from daily operations, he continues shaping the field as a mentor, speaker, and champion for accountability and compassion-driven action. In recognition of his contributions, he was named to Dog Fancy's "45 People Who Have Changed the Dog World" and received the Assisi Award from the New Zealand Companion Animal Council.

"People don't need to be fully ready to be empowered. They just need someone to believe in them. Be that person for someone else."

James Bias

Mentors, Milestones, and Mission: The Moments That Shaped Me

Looking back, I didn't follow a roadmap into animal welfare leadership. I followed moments. Moments when someone gave me a chance, when a need was bigger than my experience, or when the mission outweighed the money. I said *"yes"* a lot, even when I didn't know what I was getting into or how I would do it. That willingness to step forward shaped how I lead today.

In the stories that follow—earning the trust of a mentor who opened doors, helping launch a shelter at age 20, and leading one of the largest cruelty cases in the country—you'll see how those lessons shaped the kind of leader I became, and the kind of leader I still strive to be.

Story 1: The Mentors Who Changed Everything

When I first entered a veterinary technician program in Houston, Texas, I didn't have a clear career plan. I just knew I liked animals. I had never even been to an animal shelter, and I am not even sure I knew they existed. Animal welfare wasn't something I had considered as a profession because, frankly, I didn't know it was one.

But all that changed thanks to George Huebner, my instructor in the veterinary technical program. George saw something in me (or maybe he just saw someone willing to show up) and invited me to go through the police academy with him so we could help investigate animal cruelty cases. I had no idea what I was signing up for, but I said yes.

Back then, the police academy was a 72-hour program, a far cry from the 2,000-hour requirement it is today. (It's amazing how much our field has professionalized over the last 30 years!) Still, it was a turning point. I volunteered with a constable's office, helping to investigate cruelty cases across Harris County and around the state. By the time I finished my two-year degree, I had earned the rank of lieutenant as a reserve officer, and I was helping lead a team of 30 volunteers dedicated solely to investigating animal cruelty.

What I didn't realize then—but see clearly now—is that George wasn't just teaching me skills. He was modeling leadership. He handed his mentoring over to Kappy Muenzer, the President of Citizens for Animal Protection (CAP) in Houston, Texas. She empowered me early, trusted me with responsibility, and let me learn by doing. That experience shaped how I lead today. I still look for those moments—when a volunteer, a staff member, or even an intern shows that spark. And when I see it, I try to give them the same opportunity George and Kappy gave me: to step up, even before they feel ready.

Leadership, at its core, is about lifting others up and trusting them to rise.

Story 2: Starting a Shelter from Scratch

I was just 20 years old when CAP asked me to help open their first animal shelter, thanks to George and Kappy being on the board. They had $25,000 in the bank, no building, and one paid office person. Most people would have said no. Again, I said yes.

I was still working evenings at my dad's gas station at the time, so this wasn't a glamorous leap. I didn't know how to start a shelter. I just figured it out as I went. One day, I was eating at a burger joint when a stranger overheard me talking about looking for space to open the new shelter. He gave me his landlord's number, and a few weeks later, I walked through a lease negotiation for our first shelter location, with the help of George, Kappy and a board that took a chance on me.

I wrote and pitched a full business plan. I applied for both the part-time manager and part-time vet tech roles—because I needed full-time work—and got hired. We opened that shelter with a skeleton crew and a whole lot of heart. We eventually expanded into a strip mall. Back then, we were just trying to do whatever we could to make it work. (That was 44 years ago. Today, CAP operates an Animal Resource Center they own outright.)

That experience taught me that leadership isn't about knowing everything. It's about stepping up, taking initiative, and being willing to take the first step before the path is clear. I learned how to navigate limited resources, build community trust, and set a foundation others could build on.

Most of all, I learned that the weight of a mission can be lightened when you empower others to carry it with you.

Story 3: The Largest Seizure Case in U.S. History

In 2009, while leading the SPCA of Texas in Dallas, Texas, I got a call that would test every principle I had developed as a leader. The People for Ethical Treatment of Animals (PETA) had embedded an investigator inside a massive exotic animal broker near Arlington, Texas, and the cruelty they uncovered was staggering. More than 26,000 animals—over 500 species—were living in deplorable conditions. PETA approached us to handle the seized animals, and said they had a donor who would help fund it.

At the time, we were preparing to build a new facility and had just demolished 36,000 square feet of warehouse space. It was the only structure we had large enough to accommodate what would become the largest animal seizure in U.S. history. We would have to find another way.

I took a proposal to our board to step in and lead the case. Some members were understandably hesitant—it wasn't our jurisdiction, and it wasn't part of our planned work. But I believed in our mission, and I believed we could—and should—do it. The board approved it, and everything came together quickly. Volunteers and partners from across the country showed up to help. My staff, overwhelmed but determined, rose to the occasion. Then, two months into the operation, the donor PETA had lined up to pay for our work backed out. Suddenly, we were hundreds of thousands of dollars into a rescue with no external funding in place.

That moment could have broken us—but I went back to the belief that's guided me for decades: mission first, money will follow. And this time, it did. A local Dallas foundation, which had previously declined to fund our capital campaign, stepped in with emergency funding to support the rescue. Corporate donors sent truckloads of supplies. And our development team, new to this kind of crisis, mobilized like seasoned pros.

The case ultimately cost us nearly $500,000. But in the end, we broke even. We completed the rescue. And we earned national respect for how we managed an impossible situation.

That case tested every part of our system—logistics, staffing, fundraising, leadership—but it also showed us what we were capable of. Once you've handled something that massive, everything else feels manageable. After that, when a staff member came to me with a 200-animal cruelty case and asked, *"Can we do this?"* I would say, *"You handled 26,000—200 is just another day."*

Leadership in that moment wasn't about having the perfect plan. It was about staying grounded when things fell apart, offering stability to my team, and trusting that others would step up when they saw our commitment. And they did—because the mission spoke louder than the fear.

What I Know Now

It's taken decades, but here's what I've learned most about leadership.

First, people don't need to be fully ready to be empowered. They just need someone to believe in them. Be that person for someone else.

Second, strong leadership isn't about knowing everything. It's about showing up, being real, and building as you go. I didn't have all the answers when I helped open that first shelter at 20, but I had the willingness to learn, the courage to ask questions, and the drive to keep moving forward.

And third, if you lead with a mission, the rest will follow. It might not be easy, and it might not happen right away, but if your heart's in the right place, the support will come.

Leadership doesn't always arrive with a title or a plan. Sometimes it shows up as a moment, and if you're willing to take the leap, that moment can shape the rest of your life.

***James Bias,** a vision-driven leader for more than four decades, has served as Executive Director of the Connecticut Humane Society (CHS) in Newington, Connecticut, since 2020. Working with the board, staff, building committee, and design team, he oversaw the replacement and relocation of an aging Pet Resource Center in Fairfield County, Connecticut. Opened in August 2025, the new Pet Resource Center offers sheltering, education, and community medical services focused on keeping pets and families together. Along with CHS's Hartford County and New London County centers, the new campus strengthens the organization's 138-year mission.*

Prior to this, Bias served as President & CEO of the SPCA of Texas in Dallas. There, he oversaw the design, construction, and opening of a modern animal care center built to meet evolving community needs, while also managing the organization's other facilities, three animal hospitals, mobile units, and public spay/neuter and wellness initiatives in partnership with multiple animal welfare organizations in Dallas.

Earlier in his career, as Executive Director of the San Antonio Humane Society, Bias spearheaded the development of a new state-of-the-art animal shelter that transformed the organization's capacity to serve the community, expanding adoptions and humane education programs and improving its ability to respond to cruelty and hoarding cases.

Previously, Bias also served as Animal Services Manager for the City of Albuquerque in New Mexico, and Executive Director of the Humane Society of North Texas in Fort Worth. His leadership skills have been honed through managing multi-site shelters and clinics, overseeing new facility construction, leading successful capital campaigns, advancing legislation, and expanding shelter operations, veterinary care, outreach, and education programs.

Bias is deeply committed to giving homeless pets a fresh start and helping families keep the pets they love—a dual focus that reflects his belief in building humane, resilient communities. He and his wife, Jennifer, share their home with two dogs, five cats, and several backyard chickens. In his spare time, he enjoys woodworking and hiking.

"Leadership isn't just about policies and procedures. It's about giving people something to hold onto when things get tough."

7

Robert Bremer

From Client to Catalyst: Leading Change from the Inside Out

I never expected to lead an animal shelter, but maybe that's what makes this journey even more meaningful.

I started my career in the military, serving as a bridge engineer and combat engineer in the Louisiana National Guard. I was building bridges and blowing things up—not exactly skills with a clear civilian application. After my service, I bounced around, working retail jobs while studying English literature. I didn't have a plan until I saw a job posting for an animal control officer. It said, "*Work with animals.*" That was enough for me to apply.

From Shelter Client to Shelter Leader

My first experience with the shelter I now lead (St. Tammany Parish Department of Animal Services in Lacombe, Louisiana), wasn't even as an employee; it was as a struggling pet owner. My dog, Pan (named after the Greek god), had gone missing. After weeks of searching, animal control picked him up, scanned his microchip, and called me. I was relieved—until I walked into the shelter and was hit with judgment and fees I couldn't afford. I had to borrow from friends to get Pan back. That memory still sits with me, and it shapes the way I lead today.

When I applied for the animal control officer job years later, I didn't realize it was the same shelter. I got the job and dove in.

I stayed for two years and was eventually promoted to Animal Control Supervisor. That's when I started thinking more strategically—not just about day-to-day calls, but about the image of animal control itself. People didn't see us as helpers; they saw us as enforcers, or worse—villains. I knew we had to change that narrative.

→ *Sometimes past struggles can help shape compassionate leadership.*

Changing the Narrative

We were operating in a high-intake, high-kill, reactive system. But I knew—and saw daily—that our officers were compassionate, hardworking people trying to do the right thing. The narrative didn't match the reality. I started capturing videos of our team rescuing animals on iPhones and posted them on social media. The response was overwhelming. People said, *"I didn't even know you did that."* Slowly, we started shifting the narrative.

Eventually, I became interim director, and later, the official director. The biggest issue we faced as a municipal shelter was space-based euthanasia. I didn't want to warehouse animals, but I also wasn't willing to euthanize simply because we ran out of room. In 2023, we made a bold decision to shift from relying on rescue transport to building a culture of local adoption. It wasn't popular at first, but it proved effective. Our local adoptions increased by 70%.

→ *Highlighting the shelter and staff's good work builds trust and shifts perception.*

Culture Change is Everything

I believe the future of animal sheltering depends on cultural change—not just within shelters, but in communities. Our motto is to be a beacon of light for the rest of Louisiana. We want to demonstrate to other shelters, especially in rural or under-resourced areas, that it's possible to build something sustainable and lifesaving. If we can do it, they can too.

Leadership to me isn't about being the smartest person in the room. It's about stepping back and letting others lead in their area of expertise. I hire people who are smarter than I am, especially when it comes to medical decisions. I don't override our veterinarian. I trust her. I don't undermine my supervisors—I encourage them to understand the systems and act autonomously with good, data-driven decisions at the heart of every policy.

Leadership also means visibility and inspiration. If you can't inspire people, you're just managing them—and that's not enough. I walk and clean the kennels. I check in face-to-face. I ask, "*What's going on in your world? How are you doing?*" I want every team member to feel seen and supported.

→ *Trusting experts and being visible inspires meaningful change.*

Lighting the Way

That focus on emotional connection has shaped our culture. I talk about lighthouses a lot. It's become my metaphor and our symbol for keeping the faith—a beacon of safety and guidance through stormy seas. I also talk about keeping the fire burning. I tell my team, "*If your flame starts to dim, lean on someone whose spark is still strong.*" (Yes, they do tease me about my use of metaphors.)

In this work, hope matters. Leadership isn't just about policies and procedures. It's about giving people something to hold onto when things get hard.

There's a quote I love from *The Leader's Greatest Return* by John C. Maxwell: "*You know you're a good leader when you create good leaders.*" That line has stayed with me. One of the proudest moments of my career wasn't a big grant or policy shift. It was watching two of my staff members go on to lead shelters and teams of their own. That's leadership. It's not about building your own legacy; it's about building others up so they can lead too. We need more leaders in animal welfare. We need it to be a discipline.

→ *Inspire with purpose. Emotional connection fuels resilience and keeps teams moving forward.*

Standing with the Front Line

If there's one thing I've learned along the way, it's that animal sheltering is deeply connected to human struggle. People often say animal issues aren't as important as human ones, but I see them as interwoven and connected. When someone is facing a financial crisis, their pet is immediately at risk. Even people who say they would never give up their animal might feel forced to when they believe they can't provide proper care.

In those moments, they turn to us. They reach out to shelters and rescues—anyone who might help. We *have* to be a safety net for both animals and their families. There is simply no quarter for complacency in contemporary animal sheltering. To help animals, you have to help people. Sometimes that's education, sometimes it's confiscation, but almost always it needs to be done with compassion.

Our animal control team brings in 45% of the 4,000 animals in our care. They see the worst—hoarding, cruelty, dogfighting—we all know those stories. They operate in a gray area: heroes to some, villains to others. I've been in their shoes. That's why I walk with them. I make sure they know I've got their backs. Our care and clinic teams take care of every single one of these animals year-round. We must have the backs of our guys and gals on the front lines—lest we forget what this job of public animal care and control is all about: helping pets and people—and that includes our own people!

→ *Leadership means standing with your people, especially when the work is hard. Our shelter can't thrive unless our team does, too.*

***Robert Bremer** has worked in animal welfare for more than a decade, beginning his career in animal control and rising to become the Director of St. Tammany Parish Department of Animal Services in Lacombe, Louisiana, in 2021. A military veteran, he brings the discipline and adaptability of his service as a combat engineer Into the often unpredictable world of animal sheltering. His leadership philosophy blends compassion, creativity, and candor with a deep commitment to culture change, both within shelters and in the communities they serve. Under his leadership, St. Tammany Parish Animal Services has transformed from a space-based, high-intake system to a lifesaving* *model that emphasizes local adoptions, community trust, and staff empowerment.*

Bremer is passionate about shifting the narrative around animal control from "enforcement" to "helping," ensuring his team is seen for the compassion and dedication they bring to the job. He believes leadership is about building others up, and he is most proud of seeing members of his staff go on to lead shelters of their own.

Bremer lives in the swamps of Lacombe, Louisiana, with his wife Ashley, daughters Grayce and Everly, and a motley crew, he says, of adopted dogs and cats.

"When you create and share a worthy vision and guide your team toward it, you're giving your team the opportunity to be part of something meaningful and important, something bigger than ourselves."

8

Bonney Brown

From Vision to Impact: Six Lessons that Stuck

Leadership in animal welfare isn't just about policies, programs, or protocols—it's about people. The people you guide, the communities you inspire, and the lives—both animal and human—you impact every day. I've had the privilege of leading through change, challenge, and transformation, and I know how hard it can be to carry the weight of responsibility while still striving to do more and be better. This reflection is a collection of lessons that helped me along the way—ideas that I hope will support and inspire you as you take on the vital work of leading others to save lives and make meaningful, lasting change.

1. Set a Big, Inspiring Goal

"Make no small plans, they have no power to stir the soul."
— Daniel Burnham, American Architect and Urban Planner

When you create an exciting, big, worthwhile goal for your organization it will inspire people to invest energy, time, and resources into making it a reality.

For my shelter, the goal was to create a no-kill community (or if you prefer, a lifesaving community)—where across our entire county, animals would only be euthanized when necessary to prevent irreparable suffering or in cases of dangerous dogs that were not safe to adopt into the community.

Your big goal also serves as a decision-making guide. There are an endless number of nice things that you could do, so to avoid getting spread too thin, you need to make smart decisions—selecting the ideas that will bring you closer to the big goal and avoiding those that will not.

2. Communicate Effectively with the Team

"The single biggest problem in communication is the illusion that it has taken place." *—George Bernard Shaw, Playwright*

Once you have created this exciting goal, be sure your staff and volunteers know about it. Communicate the goal in a way that makes it real, understandable, and inspiring. You want others to be able to see it and feel it.

Be sure team members understand the goal and how their role—whether cleaning, adoption counseling, or bookkeeping—is a crucial part of achieving it. Every job is important, and everyone needs to be pulling in the same direction.

Setting clear expectations will help staff and volunteers make the right decisions. We did this by providing guidelines for staff to follow when making decisions. We defined and communicated these priorities:

→ Create lifesaving solutions for the animals.

→ Involve the community in our work.

→ Deliver quality customer service.

→ Provide excellent care to the animals.

How can you be sure the message is received as intended? Ask people to share their understanding and impressions back to you in their own words.

3. Engage Your Community in the Goal

"Do good work, tell people about it, then ask them to help." *— Richard Avanzino, Former President of Maddie's Fund*

Back in the 1990's, Richard Avanzino, then President of the San Francisco SPCA, laid out this high-level road map for building a base of support, and it still works today.

→ Do good work. Be the best you can be, save lives.

→ Tell people about it. Share stories about the animals you helped with the public.

→ Ask them to help. Ask the public to help save more animals and achieve the big goal by donating, volunteering, and adopting.

At its heart, fundraising is about relationships, which are built through effective communication. Social media is powerful, but if it is your primary means of communicating with the public, you're missing many potential supporters. Diversify your communication strategies and you'll reach a larger audience of animal lovers.

Gratitude is a sure-fire way to deepen your relationship with supporters. Thanking your donors and volunteers with sincerity and in a way they prefer is golden.

Let volunteers really contribute. They can do great things, but if your organization relegates volunteers to only limited, simple tasks, you and the animals are missing out.

Regarding one-on-one communications with the public, we banished the words: "It's our policy." These words aim to shut down communication; they are inflexible, unhelpful, and lack empathy. They are also infuriating to the person on the receiving end. People and animals are more important than rigid policies, so we encouraged staff to focus on what we could do to help, to be creative problem solvers, and to ask a manager before declining a request.

4. Think Differently About Challenges

"Obstacles don't have to stop you. If you run into a wall, don't turn around and give up. Figure out how to climb it, go through it, or work around it." *—Michael Jordan, Hall of Fame basketball player*

It's not uncommon for people facing a sudden challenge to fixate on the reasons why it cannot be done. This natural response is disempowering, so my colleague Diane Blankenburg has a great way of turning this on its head. Diane asks, *"What can we do?"* Instead of a downward spiral into what we cannot do, Diane gets everyone thinking and talking about what we can do, and the discussion turns to potential solutions.

Some real-life examples of situations I have seen Diane get her team to bring their best energy to include: 45 cats that needed a speedy rescue from a bad situation, raising $5,000 for crucial equipment quickly, and neutering 800 animals in a rural community within a few weeks' time.

Diane gets people focused on potential actions that will help, and there is a lot of power in that. Action and determination attract the right people (staff, volunteers, donors) and resources (funds) to your organization. There's nothing more empowering than overcoming a challenge and nothing more powerful than success in attracting more successes. You can give your team the confidence that together we can do what is needed.

5. Be Creative

"In the beginner's mind, there are many possibilities, but in the expert's mind there are few." *—Shunryu Suzuki, Zen Buddhist monk and teacher*

Of course, we want to acquire expertise, but we also need to keep part of our minds open to creative new solutions.

One example is the conception that capacity is an immovable barrier to saving move lives. Instead, you can view capacity as something that can be expanded to meet demand rather than disempowering the team by letting your current capacity become a self-imposed, self-fulfilling limitation.

There are plenty of ways shelters can expand their capacity—adopt pets out more quickly by aggressively and creatively marketing pet adoptions, actively recruiting more foster homes, creating a more efficient flow to get animals ready for adoption, developing programs to help keep pets in homes, and raising more funds by telling the community about the animals you need help saving. I am sure that several of you reading this will come up with more ideas to expand your capacity, maybe ideas no one else has dreamed of yet!

Some of the biggest and most important innovations in animal sheltering were considered radical ideas at first because they flew in the face of the best practices of their time. Some were even vigorously resisted only to eventually be accepted as a best practice that would revolutionize sheltering.

Juvenile spay/neuter, trap-neuter-return (TNR), flexible adoption policies, free adoptions, rejecting euthanasia as a primary means of population control—these are just a few of the ideas that questioned the conventional wisdom of the times. Each of these concepts only took hold because someone came up with them, tried them, and shared their successes even when they were not immediately embraced by everyone.

To attract the best and the brightest to shelter leadership we need to keep the creativity and innovation in sheltering—value the ideas of staff and leaders working in shelters along with the contributions of experts. You or someone on your team could be the person to come up with the next big lifesaving innovation!

6. Truly lead

"A leader takes people where they want to go. A great leader takes people where they don't necessarily want to go, but ought to be." *—Rosalynn Carter, former First Lady of the United States*

Leadership is an ongoing challenge, and it can be tempting for would-be leaders to avoid some of the most difficult aspects of it.

Sometimes would-be leaders think that leadership is primarily about consensus building. That's a valuable skill, but it's not a substitute for leadership, which includes creating a clear vision for the team of what we can accomplish together that will really make a difference for the animals and our community.

When you create and share a worthy vision and guide your team toward it, you're giving them the opportunity to be part of something meaningful and important, something bigger than themselves. A well-articulated vision can create unity of purpose, the drive to achieve something great, and can compound the impact of everyone's efforts.

Sometimes, people hesitate to lead because they fear not being liked. Faith Maloney, one of the founders of Best Friends Animal Society, had great advice for this: *"In managing people, aim for respect over liking. Liking is transient, today they like you, tomorrow you have to ask them to do something differently, and they don't like you so much. Respect is more enduring."*

In addition to creating an inspiring vision and earning the respect of teams, as a leader you can inspire action, drive progress, and ensure the desired results are achieved.

When your team accomplishes more than they imagined they ever could, you, their leader, will have given them something very valuable—a sense of accomplishment, the satisfaction and warm glow of success that comes only from making a real difference in the world.

***Bonney Brown** is the President and Co-Founder of Humane Network, a national consulting organization that helps animal welfare organizations and animal services agencies succeed with less stress. She also co-founded Options Veterinary Care, a nonprofit clinic in Reno, Nevada, and helped create the first online Animal Shelter Management Certificate Program through the University of the Pacific, where she teaches.*

Brown previously served as executive director of the Nevada Humane Society, where she led an open-admission shelter that annually housed more than 16,000 animals and helped achieve a 94% communitywide save rate. She also held national leadership roles at Best Friends Animal Society and Alley Cat Allies, where she worked on lifesaving programs, communications, and advocacy.

An accomplished writer, Brown has authored numerous articles on fundraising, marketing, and shelter management, and was a columnist for the Reno Gazette-Journal and Animal Sheltering Magazine.

Between 2020 and 2022, Brown co-hosted the "Shelter Success Simplified" podcast alongside Mark Robison.

Brown's work has earned multiple national honors, including the Maddie's Fund Community Lifesaving Award, the ASPCA Henry Bergh Award for exceptional leadership, and recognition as Shelter Director of the Year. She holds a Bachelor of Fine Arts degree from Boston University in Boston, Massachusetts.

Adopt
Me

"Animals don't judge us, and we shouldn't judge the people who come to us either."

Kerri Burns

Why Trust, Listening, and Letting Go Matter

I didn't grow up dreaming about a career in animal welfare. In fact, I didn't even know it was a career path. My background is a bit of everything—social work, car sales, disaster response, even police work. But once I found my way into this field, I knew I was home.

Still, it took time for me to grow into the leader I am today. I had to learn that leadership isn't about knowing everything or doing everything yourself. It's about knowing who you are, being honest about where you're not strong, and building a team that complements your skills and fills in the gaps. There's no room for ego in this work. And there's no success without trust.

The Power of the Pause

One of the most important lessons I've learned through the years is to slow down. In this field, everything can feel like a crisis. And sometimes it is, but not usually. Taking a few extra moments to ask questions and truly listen can significantly impact the outcome of a situation.

A man once pulled into our parking lot in a big truck with two happy, tail-wagging dogs. He came inside and said, *"I need to surrender one of my dogs."* That's all. He didn't say why. Some places might have taken the dog and moved on, no questions asked. But our staff paused. They sat with him. They listened. For 30 minutes, he repeated himself, clearly struggling with a problem he seemed embarrassed to share. Finally, it came out; he couldn't afford to feed both dogs and had to give one up. *Imagine having to make that choice!* That's not an animal problem. That's a people problem.

So, we gave him a bag of dog food. We told him to come back whenever he needed more. That's why we're here, not just to help pets, but help the people who love them. Grateful, he left in tears with both dogs still by his side. That moment stuck with me. Because what we really gave him wasn't food; it was dignity, and a reminder that he wasn't alone.

That story plays out in different ways every day. My team is trained to take the time to listen and reflect. To ask, *"How do we get to "yes?"* Even if the answer is, *"We can't help, but here's someone who can."* Animals don't judge us, and we shouldn't judge the people who come to us either.

That approach to leadership came from experience. I used to carry everything on my shoulders. Every problem felt personal. I lost sleep. My health suffered. What finally changed? I started listening better—really listening. I realized that most people don't say what they mean right away. There's usually one word, one sentence buried in their story that tells you what's really going on. If you can find that, you can lead with empathy. You can guide a situation rather than just react to it.

That shift—from reactive to proactive—changed not just how I lead, but how I live.

Trust Your Staff to Make Decisions

Compassion doesn't mean saying "yes" to everything. It means knowing your mission, equipping people to make thoughtful decisions, and trusting them to do so. At Santa Barbara Humane (in Goleta, California), every new staff member is trained across departments before they're placed in a specific role. They learn how the entire organization operates, not just their specific area.

We also give them an *Empowerment Card*—a simple but powerful tool with six questions:

1. Is it legal?
2. Does it align with our mission?
3. Is it in the best interest of the animal or person?
4. Is it good customer service?

5. Am I the best person to make this decision?
6. Does it need to be made right now?

In any given situation, if they can answer "yes" to these six questions, they don't need to ask me for help or permission. They can act because we've trained them and trust them.

I try to model that trust in the way I take vacations. I tell my staff, *"If the building is on fire, call the fire department."* Otherwise, there is generally nothing so urgent it can't wait until I return. I trust they can handle things while I am away. I also encourage them to do the same when they are away from work or on vacation. I want them to be able to step away, detach, and know we have things well in hand until they return. Because burnout is real, and if we don't protect our energy, we can't be here for the long haul.

Build the Future by Building Up People

When I joined Santa Barbara Humane in 2018, we were doing about ten adoptions a month. We had no donor database, no central records, and a website that barely functioned. Staff were using a patchwork of email platforms—AOL, Yahoo, Gmail—take your pick.

Today, we've merged with the second-largest humane organization in the area, launched a capital campaign, rebuilt our infrastructure, and established a team and culture that can support more than 2,000 adoptions annually. That growth didn't come from money. It came from people.

From the beginning, I've believed that if we want animal welfare to be seen as a professional field, we have to treat it like one—and that means investing in the people who make it work. We offer more than just jobs. We offer pathways to learn, grow, and lead, no matter what your title.

We've become a teaching hospital for veterinary students. Some rotate through, fall in love with the culture, and come back to join us full-time. We cover the costs of staff pursuing certifications, taking Registered Veterinary Technician (RVT) exams, or enhancing their skills in animal behavior and training. We cover conference registration fees and encourage attendance, not just for managers but for anyone who wants to learn. You can't just scoop poop all day and be expected to thrive. People need growth. They need tools and a reason to stay.

Professional development also means creating a culture of mentorship. When someone comes to me with a challenge, I don't tell them what to do. I ask: *"What are your options? What's the best outcome here? What precedent does this set?"* I want my team to slow down and think things through. To feel confident making the call, even when I'm not there. Especially when I'm not there.

That kind of leadership is about trust, not control. I recall stepping in as an interim director at a shelter where the entire executive team had been let go on the same day I arrived. The staff didn't know me, and they were angry. They assumed I was part of the reason the executive staff was let go. But I showed up every day and listened. I said, *"If you need to yell or cry, do it. I will listen. But if you can't move past what's happened and be here to help the animals, it might be time to move on—and that's okay, too."*

It took months, but eventually, we moved forward together. Because leadership isn't about fixing everything. It's not about being the loudest voice in the room. It's about creating space for people to show up fully, learn from the process, and do their best work, day after day.

Mentorship and the Ripple Effect of Leadership

If there's one piece of advice that I would give to someone in this field, it's this: start learning early. Don't wait until someone is promoted to start teaching them how to lead. Begin when you see the spark—when someone shows curiosity, initiative, or potential. Invite them to join leadership conversations. Give them small responsibilities and check in often. And most importantly, make sure you've had the tough conversations—what's working, what's not—before you move someone into a leadership position.

Leadership isn't about perfection. It's about growth. Encourage your team to think critically and act with care. Help them develop the ability to pause, assess the situation, and ask the right questions. If someone on my team is facing a tough decision and stops to ask, *"What would Kerri do,"* it's not because I have all the answers, but because they've learned how to think things through, spot the moment, and reflect before making a decision. That's when I know I've done something right by them.

Remember, this work will always be emotional. The public won't always understand it. There will always be critics. I've been attacked online by people who've never stepped foot inside our shelter. I've seen stories spun that missed the truth entirely. But I've learned to stay focused on the animals and the people we're here to serve.

I never imagined I would build a life in this field. But I'm grateful every day that I did. And I believe—wholeheartedly—that there are extraordinary people working now with the leadership potential to make this field even more compassionate, more professional, and more humane than it's ever been.

If even one person you've mentored goes on to create a kinder world for animals and the people who care for them, then your impact will ripple far beyond what you can see.

***Kerri Burns** is a respected leader in the animal welfare field with more than two decades of experience driving impact at the local and national levels. She currently serves as CEO of Santa Barbara Humane, overseeing one of California's oldest and most trusted animal organizations.*

Before joining Santa Barbara Humane, Burns served as Interim Executive Director at Tree House Humane Society in Chicago, and previously as President of the Pet Alliance of Greater Orlando. She also served as Interim CEO and President of the Humane Society of Southern Arizona in Tucson.

Burns' leadership roots run deep. She led Animal Emergency Services Programs for the American Humane Association, where she coordinated disaster response for some of the nation's most high-profile animal emergencies. She later advanced public-private collaboration as a Charitable Giving Manager at PetSmart Charities®.

Highly regarded for her ability to build strong nonprofit partnerships and elevate community-based programs, Burns has received several honors, including the American Humane Association's Dennis White Award for her educational outreach and recognition as one of the Pacific Coast Business Times' Top 50 Women in Business.

"I'll keep fighting for the animals, yes. But I will fight just as much for the people who care for them, and for the belief that we can do this better, together."

10

Donna Casamento

From Walking Dogs to Leading Change

Animal welfare isn't easy work. People often assume it's all puppy kisses and happy adoptions. But those of us in the field know better. This work is complex, emotional, and filled with both heartbreak and hope. We're not just helping animals; we're building systems, raising funds, facing trauma, and challenging outdated thinking. And while I've always had a passion for people and purpose-driven work, I never imagined the path would lead me here—or ask so much of me along the way.

I came from the worlds of financial services and nonprofit human services. I understood program management, budgets, and the human impact of organizational care. What I didn't expect was how quickly animal welfare would become my calling—and how deeply it would change me.

It started with a walk—literally. My daughter needed volunteer hours for high school, so she asked me to go with her to walk dogs at the Pet Helpers Adoption Center in Charleston, South Carolina. We were laughing, having fun, just enjoying being around the animals. I wasn't thinking about career paths or leadership at all when the founder walked up and struck up a conversation with us. She asked who we were and what brought us in. I mentioned my background in nonprofit program management, and that was all it took to spark a new direction I never saw coming.

Two weeks later, I was asked to join the staff in a part-time marketing role, which I accepted. Two months later, I became the executive director. Talk about unexpected: One minute I was volunteering with my daughter, the next I was helping lead one of the community's largest shelters. Nothing about it was planned, but everything about it felt purposeful.

I was learning everything on the job - how to administer vaccines, manage adoptions, and run a shelter - and the urgency of the work became impossible to ignore.

Shortly afterwards, I helped start one of the community's first animal transport programs for Pawmetto Lifeline in Columbia, South Carolina. At the time, that community was euthanizing 18,000 animals a year in a city of less than 200,000 people. We worked with two local counties that were at first skeptical about letting us in the door. We didn't have fosters or much money, but we had heart. We began marketing animals via email, sending messages every evening to a growing network. We actually got kicked off email platforms for sending too many emails. We had only five days to save lives, so if we hadn't sent out all these emails, many animals would not have made it.

A Breaking Point — and a Beginning

I will never forget sitting at my kitchen table, removing the names of animals that didn't make it that week from our list. My husband found me crying and said, *"This is too hard. You can't keep doing this."* And I said, *"You don't understand. I've seen it now. I can't* not *do it."* That night, I knew this would be my career path from then on.

But to this day, I struggle to push a grocery cart in the store. That's because for years, when I worked with the county shelter, they used shopping carts to move the bodies of euthanized animals. That trauma doesn't go away. It's with me and will be with me always. And I know it's with every shelter worker who has seen too much and had too little support.

Years later, when I arrived at IndyHumane in Indianapolis, Indiana, the shelter was experiencing a financial deficit and a culture of low morale. I knew change would be hard. Some staff were ready to link arms and move forward. Others preferred the old ways—warehousing animals, avoiding data, resisting transparency, and not embracing new sheltering methods.

But we didn't have the luxury of time. Our financial situation demanded urgent action, and I knew some decisions would be unpopular, not only with staff but with the public. In today's world, transparency and reform often come with online scrutiny. Early on, I sat down with the board and said, *"When I make unpopular decisions, the community will likely come after me on social media. The question is, not what will I do when that happens, but how will you support me when it does?"* It wasn't about fear; it was about trust. I needed to know that the board understood the stakes and would support leadership when tough decisions had to be made. Although some found it difficult, I was fortunate to have a board that stood by us and supported the changes we brought about.

Change management (guiding people through transitions) isn't always clean or comfortable. But it's necessary. And while it came with criticism, including death threats and petitions calling for my removal, I stood by the decisions my team and I made to move the organization forward. A well-respected colleague once told me, *"I have three petitions against me. Join the club. Sounds like you're making a difference."*

Investing in staff, helping the community

At IndyHumane, we've worked hard to build a data-driven, values-aligned organization—one that leads with transparency and accountability. Every Friday, I send a weekly report to staff and volunteers that includes admissions, adoptions, clinic numbers, enrichment updates, and photos of recently adopted pets in their new homes. We share wins, celebrate progress, and stay connected to the purpose behind the work. At the top of that email, it says, *"This is us."*

But numbers alone don't build culture. That's why I walk through the halls, check in with staff, and stay present to what they're experiencing. We have also invested in leadership development and communication training for our staff because I believe in growing people, not just measuring outcomes. That investment, combined with daily connection and consistent follow-through, has helped shift our culture over time.

When I first started at IndyHumane, staff would say, *"Hi, Donna,"* with hesitation, as if they were bracing for a correction or giving a shout-out to everyone that the CEO was watching. Today, I hear, *"Hi Donna, what's up?"*—spoken with smiles, curiosity, and a collaborative spirit. That kind of change doesn't happen overnight. It happens through trust, consistency, and showing up when it matters most.

That culture shift wasn't just internal—it also changed how we showed up for our community. As staff members began to feel more supported, they also became more empowered to support one another. We established a Pet Resource Center. One moment that stays with me was a man who showed up to surrender his cat, Rikko. He had gone to a vet, paid for the exam, but couldn't afford the $40 prescription his cat needed for a urinary tract infection. He was heartbroken.

We looked at the records, gave him the medication (which cost us $15), and sent him home with Rikko. If we had taken the cat in, we would have spent hundreds of dollars on housing and treatment. And more importantly, we would have broken up a family that just needed a little help.

This is what it means to open our doors and our hearts to support people, not just pets. When people tell me they want to work with animals because they don't like people, I immediately know they are not a good fit for this work. The work is all about helping people. People who love their pets. People who are doing their best. People who need support, not judgment.

Now, I am fortunate to have a fantastic board and the best team I have ever worked with—a team that shows up every day not only for the animals but for each other.

Advice to Emerging Leaders

If I could offer anything to those just starting, it would be this:

→ **Progress is possible.** The work is hard. But lives will be saved, and systems will evolve. Stay the course.

→ **Lead with transparency.** Communicate clearly, even when it's uncomfortable. People can handle the truth when they trust your motives.

→ **Kindness matters.** Be respectful. Don't disparage others. Don't assume your way is the only way. This field is filled with people who care deeply and work in unique ways. Respect that.

→ **Build your support system.** Have people you can turn to when the backlash comes—because if you're doing bold work, it *will* come.

→ **Take a long-view perspective.** You're not just saving animals today; you're creating a better future for animals tomorrow. Make the work sustainable and collaborative.

This work has been harder than I ever imagined, but also more meaningful than I ever hoped. And I'll keep showing up, every day, for the people and animals who count on us. Every adoption, every clean kennel, every late-night call to one of our rescue partners in need adds up to something bigger. It's not just about leadership or strategy; it's about all of us working together, whether volunteer, board member, adopter or donor. Everyone who touches this work plays a part in what we build.

So yes, I'll keep fighting for the animals. But I'll fight just as fiercely for the people who care for them, and for the belief that we really *can* do this better, together.

***Donna Casamento** is a nationally recognized leader in animal welfare, known for her innovative approach to public-private partnerships and for building sustainable, lifesaving programs. She has served in senior leadership roles across the country, including CEO of Pet Helpers in Charleston, South Carolina, Executive Director of Palm Valley Animal Society in Edinburg, Texas, and Executive Director of the Humane Society of Southwest Missouri in Springfield, Missouri, where she helped increase the live release rate from 64% to 97%. As Chief Program Officer for Michelson Found Animals, she oversaw national initiatives including the Michelson Found Animals Microchip Registry and the Los Angeles-based Adopt & Shop program.*

In 2022, Casamento joined IndyHumane as CEO following a national search. A Midwest native, she brings decades of experience to support IndyHumane's goals of increasing adoptions, expanding its Pet Resource Center to help keep pets with their families, and ensuring long-term financial sustainability. She is also a founding member of Operation Indy Animals and The Indiana Coalition of Animal Welfare Professionals, which promotes collaboration and shared learning across the state.

Casamento has collaborated with animal welfare organizations in New York, Colorado, Florida, and the Carolinas, and has served on the boards of the South Carolina Animal Care and Control Association and the South Carolina Legislative Association.

She has two adult children, one in California and the other in Florida, and lives in Indianapolis with her three cats, Bigby, Mozart, and Atticus.

"After everything I've experienced—scrappy beginnings, bold moonshots, near-death challenges, the thing I've come to believe most deeply is this: Our people are the mission, too."

Julie Castle

A Few Quarters, a Phone Call, and a Dream of Something Better

We were broke, sunburned, and grumpy. My friends and I had just finished a post-college road trip from Utah to Mexico before heading off on our respective life journeys. Mine was to begin at a prestigious east coast law school. We were making the long-haul home in my battered 1979 Dodge Colt—every panel a different color from too many fender benders, no air conditioning, and no working radio. We had just enough gas money to make it back and a few dollars left—barely enough for each of us to buy a candy bar at the next stop.

Somewhere along the way, one of my travel mates insisted we make a detour to visit an animal sanctuary in southern Utah. None of us wanted to stop. We were exhausted and just wanted to get home. But she kept begging, and we gave in.

We pulled into Angel Canyon in Kanab, Utah, and the second I stepped out of the car, I knew something was different. The place was stunning; it was so beautiful it felt sacred. But it wasn't just the land. It was the people. I met the founders of Best Friends Animal Society and heard them speak—*really* speak—about a philosophy I had never encountered before: no-kill.

They gave us a tour of the canyon and that evening, we had dinner with them. Unlike in the world of traditional animal sheltering, they weren't asking how to humanely dispose of animals. They were asking *why* we were disposing of them at all. That question—so simple, so bold—upended everything I thought I knew.

I left the canyon certain of one thing: I had to be part of this.

So, as we drove out of town, I did something every parent probably dreads. I called my dad from a pay phone. *"Hey, I'm not going to law school. I'm moving to Kanab to work at an animal sanctuary."* There was a long silence on the other end of the line. He was not thrilled. But I had never been more sure of anything in my life.

From Shock to Sanctuary

Before that trip, I had already glimpsed how bad things were in animal welfare, but I didn't fully understand it yet.

A couple of years earlier, I had tried to adopt a cat from the local shelter in my college town. It was a cinder block building on the edge of town, out near the dump. I walked in, expecting to find a few cats and someone who could help me.

But the place was eerily empty. There were rows of cages, but not a single animal. A man in cowboy boots sat at a desk with his feet propped up and a newspaper in front of him. I told him I wanted to adopt a cat. Without looking up, he said, *"Don't have any. Took care of them."*

I asked him what he meant.

He explained, almost casually, that every morning they rounded up the animals from the day before, put them in a barrel, hooked it up to an old truck's exhaust pipe, and euthanized them that way.

I remember thinking: *What decade are we in? Is this for real?*

It was. And as horrifying as it sounds, that shelter wasn't alone. This was still common practice in the early '90s.

So, when I arrived at Best Friends and heard the founders speak about building a better way—about not just saving animals, but saving our humanity—it wasn't just inspiring, it was redemptive.

A Crash Course in Grit and Heart

When I reported for work at the sanctuary in Kanab, I had no job description, no place to live, and no clue what I was doing.

I lived in my van, showered at the gym, and showed up every morning to get my assignments: repair fencing, help in Dogtown, fix the radiator on the sanctuary truck, figure out the irrigation system at Cat World. None of it came with instructions. But that was the culture. We lived by a simple phrase: *"When in doubt, figure it out."*

My first paycheck was $183.

I was employee #17.

And I loved it.

Back then, we had no marketing budget, and no strategy team. We raised money by setting up card tables in front of grocery stores in Los Angeles, Salt Lake City, San Francisco, and any city within a day's drive of the Kanab. We showed people photos of our animals, talked about no-kill, had a coffee tin for donations, and asked people for help. At night, we would fax the donor names back to the sanctuary, where one of the founders would call each one to say thank you—no matter the amount of the donation.

That's how we built our community; one human interaction at a time.

A few years in, a consultant told us we would never raise real money unless we showed suffering—starving dogs, abused cats, the kind of imagery that breaks your heart.

But that wasn't Best Friends. We weren't selling sorrow. We were building hope. We believed people didn't need to be devastated into caring. They simply needed to believe their compassion could make a difference. We showed them transformation, healing, and possibilities. And it worked. It defined who we were and who we would become.

One Conference. One Investment. A National Shift.

By the early 2000s, we began hearing from people around the country who felt isolated in their lifesaving work. Their love and caring for the animals made them feel like the odd-person-out. They thought they were the only ones who felt this way. We realized they needed a place to connect, so we created one. The *No More Homeless Pets* conference launched in 2000 with 350 attendees. Most were grassroots rescuers, and they were hungry for tools, inspiration, and each other.

Around that same time, Maddie's Fund presented us with a bold opportunity: $11 million over five years to do something truly transformative. Richard Avanzino, who had just come from the San Francisco SPCA, was the President of Maddie's Fund at the time. He was ready to take the lessons he had learned there and apply them on a national scale. We jumped at the opportunity and set a goal to take Utah to no-kill.

At the time, Utah shelters were euthanizing over 58,000 animals annually. The rescue groups, shelters, and veterinarians weren't even talking to each other, but an essential element of Rich's program criteria was to build a coalition of stake holders, so we brought everyone together—not to compete, but to collaborate. We ran outdoor advertising and opened mall-based adoption centers. We hired people who hadn't been "trained" to believe in limitations. And together, we began to prove what was possible.

That's when I realized something: Change doesn't come from better ideas. It comes from people brave enough to act on them.

Cancer, Los Angeles, and Clarity

In December 2009, my world shifted again. I was diagnosed with advanced-stage cancer. It was aggressive. The doctors at UCLA weren't sure I would survive. While undergoing treatment in Los Angeles, I had a decision to make—wallow or work. I chose to work.

From my chemo infusion chair, I began to sketch out a plan: What if we took the model that worked in Utah and used it to make Los Angeles a no-kill city?

At the time, LA was taking in 56,000 animals a year and their save rate was only 56%. We discovered that 21,000 of the animals were kittens, too young to survive in a shelter environment. We took over a city shelter slated for closure and created a kitten nursery. We pulled together every stakeholder we could find—rescue groups, government agencies, animal advocates—and began to build a coordinated plan.

That's how *NKLA*—No Kill Los Angeles—was born.

I didn't know if I had years or just months, but I knew I wanted to spend whatever time I had making a difference.

Being diagnosed with cancer in my thirties changed me. It made every day after that feel like a gift. It deepened my empathy and sharpened my focus. It reminded me that we don't have time to waste—not in life, and not in this movement.

From 2035 to 2025: A Moonshot Worth Taking

In 2016, we ran an expert analysis for the most realistic timeline for the country to achieve no-kill. The answer that came back, 2035, nearly 20-years down the road, was hardly inspiring. We could do better. We had to do better. Too many animals were dying. So, we looked at what it would take to cut five years off that projection in terms of resource allocation and made 2030 our target.

Going into our National Conference, my keynote address hinged on the goal of achieving no-kill in this country by 2030, But in 2016, that still felt like the next century. It lacked the urgency I knew we needed to catalyze change.

Shortly before walking on stage, I stared at a slide predicting that the U.S. could reach no-kill by 2030. *2030*? I could imagine the quiet doubts echoing in people's heads: *Will I even still be in this field by then? Will I still be alive?*

I pulled aside Best Friends CEO and Board Chair, both of whom were Founders, and shared my thoughts. "*We need to light a fire under ourselves and the movement and 2030 doesn't do it. I want to obligate ourselves to leverage all of our resources and our partners to commit to no-kill 2025.*" They both smiled and gave me a thumbs up.

I scrapped the slide, walked up to the mic and said: *"We're planting a stake in the ground to lead the country to no-kill by 2025."*

The crowd erupted. It was risky. It was unvetted. Some of my own team looked stunned. But it was real, and more importantly, it did light a fire.

The People are the Mission

After everything I have experienced—from scrappy beginnings, bold moonshots, and near-death challenges—the thing I have come to believe most deeply is this: Our people are the mission, too.

During COVID-19, we faced some tough choices. People weren't coming to the sanctuary to adopt—or donate. Things looked grim, and the staff was rightly worried they were about to lose their jobs. I asked our Chief Financial Officer to give me three budget scenarios. Here is what he provided:

→ Scenario A: Survival only: Massive cuts and layoffs, just enough to keep the lights on.

→ Scenario B: Reduced operations: Some programs paused, some staff let go.

→ Scenario C: Hold the line: Stay fully staffed, dip into reserves if needed, and get through this together.

He told me plainly: *"Scenario A may be our only option."*

I said, ***"We're not doing that. We are not laying people off."***

I believed—and still believe—that this was our moment to live our values, not just talk about them. If people were committing their lives to this mission, then the least we could do was commit to them. I chose Scenario C.

We reassigned employees into new roles overnight. People who couldn't do their regular jobs helped with animal care or took shifts calling donors just to check in. Others supported virtual adoptions, helped track inventory, or simply lifted team morale.

In total, we reassigned more than 150 positions across the organization.

And every single morning, I showed up on Zoom to talk with the staff. No script. No slides. Just a message: *"We're still here. The sun will rise. One foot in front of the other. We've got this."*

It wasn't about having all the answers. It was about being present. That's what culture is. Not a mission statement in a frame. Not a poster in a hallway. It's how you treat people when the pressure is on.

What Comes Next

When I used my candy bar money to call my dad from a pay phone on the side of the road, I had no idea what kind of life I was stepping into. I couldn't possibly imagine the path that was unfolding before me. All I knew was that I had found something worth following.

I never became a lawyer. Instead, I became a mechanic, a fence builder, a tour guide, a movement strategist, and eventually a CEO. I didn't step into a job. I stepped into a lifetime of believing we could be better—and doing something about it.

Today, that 2025 goal is no longer an abstraction. It's here. It's real. And yes, it's messy. We haven't solved everything. But we've saved millions of lives. We've flipped the script in city after city. And we've proven that when people come together with courage and clarity, real change happens.

What I've learned leading a movement, a mission—and myself.

1. **When in doubt, figure it out.** I didn't start with expertise. I started with a van and a willingness to learn. Leadership isn't about knowing everything. It's about showing up, getting your hands dirty, and solving what's in front of you.

2. **Hire for hunger, not history.** I looked for people who hadn't been told what wasn't possible. People who weren't already indoctrinated into "the way things have always been done." Give me grit and vision over a perfect résumé any day.

3. **Vision beats fear.** The safe bet was 2035. But I chose 2025. Big dreams push people. Safe dreams don't. If the timeline doesn't scare you at least a little, it's not bold enough.

4. **Your people are the mission, too.** Culture isn't perks. It's how you show up for your team when things get hard. During COVID,

we didn't lay anyone off. We reassigned people, checked in daily, and pulled through together.

5. Movements need momentum. A vision is powerful, but it's momentum that turns it into reality. Setting bold goals—like no-kill by 2025—gives people something to rally around. It creates urgency, sparks action and reminds us that change doesn't come from waiting. It comes from believing, stepping up, and pushing forward—together.

So, what comes next? Well, we haven't finished what we started. We stay in the fight, and we keep building a world where no animal is forgotten...and no person is told their dream is too big. Because that canyon didn't just change my life, it helped me believe in a future where *every life matters*—and every voice has the power to protect it. And along the way, we must inspire and prepare the next generation of leaders to carry this mission forward.

And as long as my feet hit the ground each morning, I'll keep walking toward that future—because every day is a gift, and the mission is far from done.

***Julie Castle** has spent nearly three decades shaping the future of animal welfare. She joined Best Friends Animal Society in Kanab, Utah, in 1996 as employee #17 and now serves as CEO, leading the national movement to make every shelter and every community no-kill. Along the way, she has never been afraid to set bold goals and rally others to achieve them.*

During her tenure as head of marketing, communications, and development, Castle helped drive a nearly 50% increase in fundraising, reaching an all-time annual revenue high of $130 million. More importantly, she positioned Best Friends as the first organization to publicly commit to taking the entire country to no-kill. Under her leadership as CEO, the U.S. shelter kill rate has dropped from 17 million pets per year in 2016 to fewer than 450,000 in 2024—a transformation powered by what she calls "scaling optimism, not guilt."

Castle is a champion for culture and innovation, believing that the best results come when staff feel empowered to lead with passion.

That philosophy has earned Best Friends national recognition, including Top Workplace USA and Fast Company's Most Innovative Company honors. InStyle Magazine recognized Castle as one of "50 Badass Women" who "show up, speak up, and get things done," and CNN featured her on Champions of Change in 2024.

Today, Castle leads a team of nearly 1,000 employees with the same conviction she's carried since the beginning: that a better world for animals is possible when people are inspired to believe—and bold enough to act. She graduated summa cum laude from Southern Utah University in Cedar City, Utah, with a double major in history and political science and a minor in communications.

"What that told me was that we had created an environment where people felt safe enough to be themselves. That was proof we were building the kind of environment where people didn't just come to work; they felt like they belonged."

Spencer Conover

Why Saving Animals Starts with Taking Care of People

In animal welfare, it's easy to focus entirely on the animals—the faces behind the kennel doors, the statistics we track, the lives we're desperate to save. But the truth is, no shelter or rescue succeeds by focusing solely on animal care. Success rises or falls on the people who show up every day: the staff cleaning kennels before sunrise, the volunteers walking dogs after work, the adoption counselors answering questions from anxious families. They are the foundation of every lifesaving achievement.

I didn't always understand that. Early in my career, I believed outcomes were everything: the save rate, the revenue, the numbers on the page. It took a humbling lesson for me to realize that the path to saving more animals runs directly through how we treat the people who care for them.

When I landed my first leadership role in animal welfare as director of operations at a large humane society, I wanted to save every single animal. I threw myself into the work, determined to succeed. Through data-driven decision-making, I helped lower expenses and raise revenue.

Two months later, I was fired.

Not because we weren't saving lives, but because nobody wanted to work with me. I had been so focused on results that I forgot the most important thing: caring for people. Losing that job was painful, but it became one of the most important leadership lessons of my career.

People, Purpose, Performance

When I joined Pasco County Animal Services in West-Central Florida, I had the chance to try again. Our county administrator at the time had a simple vision statement: *People, Purpose, Performance*. And in my best Ted Lasso impression, I thought, *Well, I like that*. And, it stuck with me.

A couple of years later, at a national conference, I heard something that shifted my perspective again. The presenter said the longest-stay resident at his shelter wasn't a dog or a cat—it was a staff member. That realization stopped me in my tracks and made me rethink leadership.

Back home, I realized our longest resident wasn't in a kennel at all—it was Troy, who had dedicated more than 30 years to the organization, serving in countless roles and touching nearly every aspect of its work. Now I knew a few things about him—that he was particular about how he liked things, that he spent his days off at the beach, and that he had just welcomed his first grandchild. But that insight from the conference prompted me to take another look. Troy wasn't just a long-standing employee—he was a person with a story, just like the 50 other staff members working alongside him. If I really wanted to make a difference, I needed to care about him and the rest of the staff as much as I cared about the animals.

Taking Care of Our People

That realization sparked changes across our organization. We began with the basics: bi-annual pay studies to ensure people were fairly compensated, regular employee surveys to ensure their voices were heard, and tuition reimbursement and continuing education to support their growth. If a staff member wanted to attend a national conference, we would find the necessary funds to support their attendance. It wasn't just about the perks. It was about proving that our people mattered and that we wanted to help them grow.

When I told Troy I planned to share his story, his eyes grew wide—he's not one for the spotlight. But when I asked if the changes we had made had helped him, he said, "*Yes, I feel like what I do actually means something now.*" That's when I knew we had given him—and others—a true sense of purpose.

Another powerful reminder came from an unexpected place. In a budget meeting, our human resources director turned to our team and said, "*Did you know there are only five openly transgender team members in all of Pasco County, and four of them work for Animal Services?*" What that told me was that we had created an environment where people felt safe enough to be themselves. That was proof we were building the kind of environment where people didn't just come to work; they felt like they belonged.

When People Thrive, Animals Thrive

When our County Administrator was preparing to leave for a new role, I asked him, "*We've taken care of our people, we've given them a purpose. When do we get to performance?*" He laughed and said, "*If you take care of those first two things, the performance takes care of itself.*"

And he was right.

Since helping our staff thrive, our average length of stay for animals dropped from 28.5 days to just 5.1 days. We reduced annual medication costs by $20,000. Animals were leaving the shelter at a faster rate than ever, and our save rate has remained above 90% since 2019, not because of a fancy building or a huge budget increase, but because we invested in our people.

So, when you see that dog who has been there the longest, give them all the love and attention they deserve, and look for every way possible to get him a home. But don't stop there. Look at who's holding the other end of the leash—the staff and volunteers who are walking alongside that animal every day. They are the ones carrying the stress and showing up every day to make a difference.

When I started in this field, I thought success was about saving every animal. What I know now is that true success comes when you care for the people who care for the animals. That's the foundation of every lifesaving achievement we've had in Pasco County. And you'll be amazed at how much lifesaving you can accomplish when you follow that simple truth—when you pour into your team, give them purpose, and create an environment where they feel valued and seen. Because when people thrive, animals thrive. And that, in the end, is what this work is all about.

Spencer Conover, (MIS), *has dedicated his career to innovative, servant leadership in animal welfare, serving at some of the nation's top organizations, including the Dumb Friends League (currently known as Humane Colorado) in Denver, Colorado, Best Friends Animal Society, the Humane Society of Utah in Murray, Utah, and Pasco County Animal Services in Land O' Lakes, Florida, where he currently serves as Assistant Director. With a strong passion for leadership development, Spencer thrives when surrounded by progressive and proactive lifesaving professionals working to transform communities for people and pets.*

Conover holds a Master of Interdisciplinary Studies in Contemporary Animal Services Leadership and Leadership Studies. He is a Certified Public Manager (CPM) and a certified Green Belt in Lean Six Sigma process improvement. Throughout his career, he has led shelter operations teams across nearly every function of animal services, including animal control, adoptions, intake, customer care, foster care, volunteer management, education and outreach, transfer and rescue, and animal behavior. He is also a Certified Animal Control Officer and holds certifications in CPR, humane euthanasia, handling dangerous and fractious animals, and Florida State Animal Response Coalition's (SARC) emergency animal handling.

In addition to his operational expertise, Conover is deeply engaged in advancing the field as a whole. He currently serves on the

Board of Directors for the Florida Animal Protection and Advocacy Association and is the President of the National Animal Care and Control Association. His professional passions include shelter operations, statistics, data-driven decision making, and the development of innovative, community-based programs that save lives and strengthen the human-animal bond.

"Stepping outside your comfort zone, even when it feels daunting, unlocks possibilities you never imagined."

Jordan Craig

Discovering My Voice: How Courage and Confidence Shaped My Leadership

I was always one of those kids who felt more at ease with animals than people. At night, my two cats and one dog would curl up on my tiny twin bed while two larger dogs snoozed on the floor nearby. They were my confidants, and I shared stories and secrets with them that were ours alone.

My connection to animals wasn't just a personal bond though, it was a family value. When I brought two cats home in my soccer bag after practice one day, my parents, despite being animal lovers themselves, made me rehome the first feline with a neighbor. With the second cat, however, they relented, understanding my determination to keep this feline for my very own.

Growing up, the responsibilities of pet ownership were passed down like a tradition, shaping how I cared for animals and respected their needs. This generational love for animals was especially evident during summers with my grandparents. Each day, we would watch *The Price Is Right*, and when Bob Barker signed off with his iconic message, *"Help control the pet population. Have your pets spayed or neutered,"* my grandma would celebrate and remind me of the importance of his words. Her enthusiasm left a lasting impression, planting the seeds of advocacy in me that would grow stronger in the years to come.

Perseverance Through Setbacks

Leaving for college was tough, especially the first year in the dorms, without any pets to keep me company. By my second year, I moved off-campus into a house where two of my roommates had dogs, but I still felt something was missing. So, I headed to the local animal shelter and adopted a cat. Overwhelmed by the choices in the communal room, I asked about a nine-month-old brown tabby named Alpha. She had just been returned by an adopter for "bad behavior," and had been at the shelter far too long. When the staff told me she didn't have much time left, I knew she was the one.

Surprisingly, though, the shelter staff didn't want me to adopt her. They said they didn't adopt to college students because too many cats had been abandoned by them. But I've always been a bit stubborn, so I wasn't taking no for an answer. They put me through every test they could think of, and I passed. I left that day with Alpha in my arms. I renamed her Pigeon, and for the next 16 years, she was my constant companion, moving with me across the country and living with me in 10 different homes.

My persistent nature carried into my professional journey as well. Although I adored my pets, I never thought I would have a career working with domestic animals. Instead, I had my sights set on working with wildlife, so I focused my college studies on primatology and animal behavior. But sometimes life has other plans. After moving to Austin, Texas, I sent my resume to the Austin Zoo, but they didn't have any openings. A board member with the zoo, however, who ran a small nonprofit shelter, saw my resume and offered me a job there instead. I was hesitant, but after months of waiting tables, I took the position. That job opened my eyes to a whole new world, and I eventually shifted my focus from wildlife to domestic animals and began looking for a position at the municipal shelter, where I found better pay and more stability.

It wasn't easy getting a job with the shelter. I applied five times over the next few months and had multiple interviews before finally landing a part-time, overnight position cleaning kennels and doing inventory. I started on Christmas Eve. I was also there to ensure the building didn't burn down in the year leading up to the shelter's move into a newly built facility across town.

Even though it was an entry-level job, I gave it my all, despite peers suggesting I was making them look less productive. I wanted to move up, so I applied for promotions repeatedly, only to face setbacks each time. After four tries, I finally got a customer service position. It took as many attempts to become a lead and then a supervisor at the shelter. But like I said, I'm a bit stubborn. I worked hard, kept applying, asked for feedback, and attended every training course the city offered.

Taking Risks and Embracing Growth

From those early beginnings, one experience stands out above all others. I was in a leadership training program, and we were divided into groups based on our personalities. We took personality tests, and they grouped us into different personality types, allowing us to learn what it was like to work with people of various types. The goal was to create a challenging dynamic. I was the youngest in the group and found myself frustrated early on as we went around in circles, with no one taking the lead. That's when it hit me. I could be the leader. I had the strongest personality and knew what needed to be done to bring everyone together. Even though I was younger than most of my peers, that "aha" moment gave me the courage to step up and be more confident in my abilities.

The risk of the unknown is terrifying, and I regularly struggle with imposter syndrome, but like anything, taking risks takes practice. I have absolutely risked and failed, but more often than not, it has been for the better. I have learned that I thrive and become more innovative under pressure. Change energizes me once I get going. I just needed the courage to get going.

Empowering Others

In addition to being persistent, I am fiercely loyal. This means I struggle when new job opportunities arise within or outside my organization. I, thankfully, share my life with a partner who is brave and always challenging me to push myself when I may want to stay in my comfort zone. Without his support and encouragement, I would not have taken the many chances I finally took along the way.

Looking back, I see a theme of perseverance and determination in my career. Every setback taught me to push harder and find solutions. Now, as a leader in my field, I am committed to fostering that same spirit in my team—creating an environment where everyone has the chance to grow, challenge themselves, and the courage to believe in themselves.

For emerging leaders, my story underscores the power of persistence, adaptability, and the courage to embrace growth. In my case, my career started with my love of animals, but it was perseverance through challenges and a willingness to take risks that drove meaningful progress in my career.

Setbacks are not failures; they are stepping-stones to building resilience and gaining invaluable insights that drive growth and progress. Stepping outside your comfort zone, even when it feels daunting, unlocks possibilities you never imagined. As leaders, our role is to cultivate an environment where others can thrive—where growth, courage, and collaboration are not just encouraged but expected. That's what I strive to do every day: build a space where my team feels empowered to take chances, reach their potential, and grow into the future leaders our field needs.

***Jordan Craig** is a changemaker in the animal welfare field, known for turning bold ideas into sustainable, lifesaving programs. As Chief Operating Officer at Operation Kindness in North Texas, she leads a powerhouse portfolio of initiatives that save more lives and strengthen shelter systems, building partnerships, mentoring local teams, delivering on-site and transport-based medical support, coordinating public services like vaccination clinics and surgeries, supporting emergency response efforts, and running an Adoption Center and Lifesaving Hub that keeps animals moving toward homes instead of languishing in kennels.*

Before joining Operation Kindness, Craig served as Executive Director of Spay Neuter Network, overseeing programs in the Dallas-Fort Worth area and San Antonio, Texas. During her tenure, she significantly expanded the organization's impact, opening a new clinic in San Antonio and launching a transport program there, building a new, expanded facility in Dallas, and strengthening regional collaborations to prevent shelter overcrowding and support underserved pet owners.

Craig's leadership spans both nonprofit and government-run animal shelters, with a consistent focus on improving quality of life for animals and their families. Building on that foundation, her unique blend of hard data and hands-on compassion has driven innovative solutions that meet community needs in lasting ways. Today, she is a sought-after speaker at national and regional conferences, sharing her expertise on using data and automation to enhance operations, improve workflows, and dismantle systemic barriers to progress. She also serves on the board of Texas Unites, which produces the state's largest animal welfare conference.

With a rare blend of operational precision, deep compassion, and strategic vision, Craig continues to shape more humane and effective systems of animal care across Texas and beyond.

"Strong leaders recognize that younger generations aren't lowering the bar; they're raising new standards for balance, fairness, and self-care. When we respect those values instead of resisting them, we create workplaces where both people and animals thrive."

14

Todd Cramer

Fine Wine or Skunky Beer? Leading with Value at Every Stage of a Career

Every leader faces a choice: to grow richer with time, like a fine wine, or to cling to outdated ways of working until we go stale, like that forgotten beer at the back of the fridge.

Through *AAWA's Diversity, Equity, and Inclusion (DEI) Ambassador Program* and *Companions and Animals for Reform and Equity's Racial Equity, Diversity, and Inclusion* bronze and silver certifications, I learned about unconscious bias. These are subconscious biases we all have towards others, shaped by a variety of factors, including the environmental and social conditioning we experienced during our upbringing. The self-examination these programs foster is invaluable, especially for someone like me, who is an avid consumer of self-help material in any format. As I looked inward to explore, honor, and own my own biases, I uncovered a surprising struggle: aging.

Personally, I've embraced aging. It has been a rite of passage for me. The migration of hair from the places I want it to the places I don't (ear hair dreads, anyone?), the extra pounds, the inability to sleep, the bad knees, the forgetfulness, and the all-around slower pace have been well-earned. These are offset by a clearer sense of who I am, valuing quality of friendships over quantity; the confidence to take risks—like learning to ride a motorcycle at 49; being loved by the best group of nieces, nephews, and great-nieces and nephews a guy could ask for; and the many other joys that aging can bring.

Professionally, however, aging hasn't come so easy. I've struggled with understanding the needs of a younger workforce. As a Gen X-er, I can relate to the internet meme that describes us as *"raised on hose water and neglect."* We were outside first thing in the morning and let back in when the streetlights came on. We were independent, and we took care of our own needs. We were taught to do as we were told the first time—or else. So, when I was new to the workforce, I showed up for work when I didn't feel well because I was being counted on and didn't want to disappoint my peers. I came in on my day off to cover for a sick colleague because I thought that is what it meant to be a team player. I didn't expect to be paid extra every time I was asked to do a little extra because I was taught that is how you get your next promotion and larger paycheck.

So, naturally, it was frustrating when I didn't perceive younger folks living these same values. But I've learned that living by those same rules doesn't work in today's workplace—and it's unfair to expect it of the younger and brilliant minds we work with now.

Good leaders shouldn't expect every generation to share their same values or work habits. Instead, they should adapt, listen, and recognize that learning goes both ways. Each generation has something to teach the other, and together we move the mission forward.

Being Valued at Every Stage of a Career

I sometimes struggle with feeling relevant at this stage in my career. I've caught myself saying to myself, *"I was somebody once,"* as I reminisce about career highlights: being the first male, youngest, and least experienced member of the ASPCA's National Shelter Outreach team at a time when the ASPCA's *Animal Precinct* television show was on-air, and National Shelter Outreach was considered the gold standard for shelter support. I was also one of the first members of the ASPCA's disaster response and forensic investigations teams. And, I developed an open adoption workshop during my time at PetSmart Charities that so impressed a board member that I was sent on the road to deliver it at national and regional conferences (my pet-sitting costs nearly broke me, but I digress). I also led the successful effort to save Luna—a dog wrongfully deemed dangerous and ordered euthanized—by rallying the board, staff, volunteers, and community, and by designing the strategy that ultimately saved her life.

Looking back, I know I've accomplished meaningful work. Admittedly, by choice, I've often served in senior supporting roles that afforded me less visibility and a more subdued voice, but even when serving in the most senior and visible role, newcomers don't always show interest in my history or experience. I often feel younger generations see me as a dinosaur—or think I got this job just because I look good sitting behind a desk (which is flattering, but wildly inaccurate)—without realizing how much experience I bring to the table.

Technology is challenging, too. Instant messaging systems like Slack are not instant for me (*can we go back to using walkie-talkies?*), and a modern generation's need for process (*can we just make stuff happen without needing an SOP first?*) creates more work in my mind (*Nike's "Just Do It" anyone?*). I can still find paper files faster, and know they are the correct version than working through an electronic system. I could go on, but I have a word count to stick to, and I write like I talk—too much.

As we age, it's easy to feel our relevance fading, and truthfully, that can be hard to face. But aging in this field doesn't mean fading away. Our experience remains a powerful asset if we're willing to adapt, share wisely, and keep learning alongside the next generation. And if young leaders remember to recognize the value of those who have been around for a while, we can bridge generations and move the field forward together.

Even now, I try to embrace those who come after me, just as I've learned from those who came before me. My close friend, and Irish Father, Joel, is a 25-year-old man in an octogenarian body. He has taught me that age truly is just a number. He is living fully, even when it means doing things differently and a bit more slowly. He is sharp and can cut through bullshit faster than a hot knife through butter. We met when he was a donor to an organization I worked for, and we became friends because he embraced a younger generation—one that included me. Joel wanted to know what I thought and believed. He has taken my advice numerous times. But I also benefit from his lived experiences and can't imagine not having him in my life. Joel has never tried to force his experiences and wisdom on me, either. Rather, he waits for me to come to him.

Because of his leadership style, I, as a leader, try to resist the urge to vomit my knowledge and share tales of my very cool career experiences with my younger staff. I let them come to me for counsel, as Joel did with me. And, if I feel a strong need to share, I ask for their permission first by simply saying, *"May I share a story with you?"* Because of Joel, I learned to solicit opinions and advice from people of all ages. And not just the selected few staff I know best or am most comfortable with. In fact, some of the most useful thoughts and opinions I've gotten have come from team members who keep to themselves and *"fly under the radar."* We should all strive to be like Joel.

Leaders must be generous with their wisdom but also humble enough to invite questions and let others seek guidance when they're ready.

Reframing Values for a Changing Workforce

In the same vein, I want to be validated just like anyone else. I may not be an OG[1], but I am not new, either. I still have a lot to offer, even if I don't always reference my experience unless someone asks.

Strong leaders also know not to overlook those who have been around longer. There's often wisdom, perspective, and lived experience that can benefit the whole team. Don't underestimate an older

1 OG—short for "Original Gangster." Today, it means someone authentic, experienced, and often a trailblazer: the kind of person whose perspective comes from years of lived experience. By that definition, Todd is more of an OG than he thinks, and his "experienced" voice adds real value to this conversation.

person simply because they may be technology-averse. I remember looking up information in the shelter management software while a younger team member stood over my shoulder. I could sense their impatience at my pace and handed over the computer mouse as I said, *"Here, you can drive."* They had the information on the screen lickety-split, and I felt a bit judged. I couldn't resist countering with, *"Don't think I don't know what just happened here. Trust me when I tell you I'm the guy you'll be looking for when the power goes out."*

If you want to lead, it's important to know that mentorship works both ways. Leaders must accept that younger generations may excel in areas we struggle with—and that's a strength to value, not a threat—even if it is a little embarrassing for us elders. But also know that we have wisdom and perspective to share in return. When both sides lean in, everyone grows stronger.

Balancing History with Progress

When pet intake levels increased during the COVID-19 pandemic and shelters that once transferred pets to other shelters faced the possibility of euthanizing pets to make room for more, it was webinars and conversations, often led by the newer, younger generation of leaders, that discussed solutions. It seems the animal welfare wheel is often reinvented when much of the work has already been done, albeit in a different format. If you want to address the intake crisis, ask the animal welfare leaders who have been around for a while, especially those long retired, about how they did it. They were managing space to prevent euthanasia decades before many of us came along.

If we want to keep moving forward as a field, we need to value both perspectives: the experience of those who have lived through past crises and the fresh ideas of younger leaders tackling today's challenges. We all benefit when we see the characteristics of younger generations as evolution, not regression. Today, using allocated sick time as the benefit it is, isn't a team member taking advantage of or being lazy; it's someone having the courage to take care of themselves and recognizing that being a walking fomite isn't cool. Not giving up a needed day off to cover for a colleague isn't being lazy or showing a lack of teamwork; it's responsibly managing obligations, practicing self-care, and prioritizing family. Being unwilling to do more for less is knowing your value and having the courage not to be taken advantage of. As the proverbial dinosaur in the room, I've learned that reframing differences into points of connection is what helps me stay relevant—and avoid extinction. I use my sick time now, and I don't apologize for not checking email after hours. For that shift in perspective, I have my younger colleagues to thank.

Strong leaders recognize that younger generations aren't lowering the bar; they're raising new standards for balance, fairness, and self-care. When we respect those values rather than resist them, we create workplaces where both people and animals thrive.

Still Here, Still Learning

When I accepted my first role in animal welfare, I thought, *"Puppies and kitties come in and you find them homes. How hard can it be?"* I certainly didn't expect to make a career out of it. And, nearly 25 years later, I can say it remains damn hard.

Getting older in a field that seems to be getting younger by the minute isn't easy either. But I'm determined to age gracefully by embracing and learning from the younger generations, and knowing my experience (*a kind word for aging don't you think?*) brings something valuable to the work too. I'm still here, still learning. I'm far from done yet.

Of course, I may cling to some old habits, but I'm still open to learning plenty of new tricks.

Now, get off my lawn.

Todd Cramer *Todd Cramer currently serves as President of the Rhode Island SPCA (RISPCA) in Warwick, Rhode Island - the state's oldest and largest humane organization - where he leads the organization's strategic initiatives to expand access to care, support pet retention, strengthen community partnerships, and perform Humane*

Law Enforcement across the state. In this role, he brings more than two decades of leadership experience in animal welfare, community engagement, and nonprofit management.

Prior to joining the RISPCA, Cramer was the Chief Operating Officer of the Potter League for Animals in Middletown, Rhode Island, where he led daily operations and human resources activities across three locations, including the spay-and-neuter clinic, low-cost veterinary clinic, and animal care center. He has also led organizations in New York and New Jersey.

At the national level, Cramer served as Senior Program Manager of Adoptions at PetSmart Charities, where he developed and supported adoption programs nationwide. He also spent several years at the ASPCA as Director of Community Initiatives and served on the Field Investigations and Response teams, responding to large-scale cruelty cases and natural disasters across the country.

Cramer is a Certified Animal Welfare Administrator (CAWA), holds bronze and silver certifications in CARE's Racial Equity, Diversity, and Inclusion (REDI) program, and is an AAWA Diversity, Equity, and Inclusion Ambassador. He is a popular speaker at national and regional conferences, including Best Friends National Conference and Humane Society of the United States' (currently known as Humane World for Animals) Animal Care Expo. He has authored articles for Animal Sheltering Magazine on progressive topics, including open adoptions and pet-friendly housing.

Outside of his professional work, Cramer is an avid motorcyclist. He lives in rural Rhode Island with his two dogs, Ivan and Beverly, and two cats, Elsa and LB.

"Work hard, but also take care of yourself. Lead bravely, stay humble, and keep learning. Love animals, but don't forget to love people, too. Yes, they may sometimes be part of the problem, but they are always part of the solution."

Jes Cytron

From Kennel Attendant to Director: Lessons in Leadership from the Front Lines

I was about ten years old when I first felt that magnetic pull to spend my life working with animals. My dad would take me to our local humane society, and together we would wander through the kennels, visiting adoptable animals. We never brought one home—not right away, anyway—but those visits left an imprint I can still feel. It wasn't until I was fourteen that we adopted our first shelter puppy, but by then the seed had long been planted.

I didn't stumble into animal welfare by accident. I knew even as a kid that I wanted to work with animals. And as I grew older, I realized it was more than that. I wanted to help the people who loved them, too. For me, loving animals and loving people go hand in hand.

The First Job That Shaped Me

My first shelter job was as an Animal Care Technician at a limited-admission shelter in Fort Collins, Colorado. I can still recall my start date—August 13, 2013—and I can still picture the purple t-shirt I wore on my first day. My first lessons were how to clean kennels and bathe animals of every temperament. The work was physically exhausting, made even harder by the fact that there was only one kennel cleaner per shift for more than 50 dogs. And because the building had no proper drainage, cleaning meant inventing creative combinations of mops, rags, and towels.

Still, I loved it all—the animals, the staff, the volunteers, the adopters. I loved it so much that by the following year, I applied for a promotion to Assistant Manager and Foster Care Coordinator.

I didn't get the position.

My leadership at the time handled the letdown with such kindness. They told me I needed more field experience before managing people and programs. That could have been a blow to my ego, but instead I asked, *"Thank you. What can I do to get there?"*

The shelter didn't have much of a budget, but they sent me to as many continuing education opportunities as they could find—low-cost or free, local or virtual, and often on my own time. I soaked up every lesson I could, applying what I learned back on the job. I would power through my animal care duties, so I could spend the rest of my shift shadowing the front desk or adoptions team. Eventually, my manager started training me to work at the desk myself.

Soon, I was covering shifts at the front desk, loving the new perspective and the extra time with the person who had gotten the promotion I had once wanted. I learned from her—from everyone—by asking for advice, coaching, and feedback. And, I was grateful even when the feedback stung.

One year later, the same position opened up again. This time, I was ready. And I got it.

The Rewards and Risks of Leadership

At 24, I suddenly had up to eight direct reports, managed a foster program with over 120 volunteers, and still ran front desk operations five days a week. I was determined to prove myself, but that determination manifested in unsustainable work habits, which, unfortunately, were rewarded in ways all too familiar in our field.

I coordinated the foster program from home at 6:00 a.m. and stayed late every night to answer emails, conduct foster inspections, and onboard new hires. It earned me recognition, and in 2017, I became shelter manager, supervising everyone except the Executive Director and grooming team.

But it came at a cost. My weeks stretched to 70 to 80 hours (which is easy to do in this field). My personal life shrank. My health issues flared, and new ones emerged. I knew my body well enough to see where this was heading, and that I needed to make a change before it became career-ending.

I also knew I wanted two things: to move into an open admission shelter and to relocate to Denver with my partner. Then the pandemic hit, accelerating everything.

A Bigger Stage, A Healthier Balance

In 2020, I was offered the chance to run the behavior and transfer programs at one of the largest open-admission shelters in Colorado and the Rocky Mountain region—Humane Colorado (formerly known as the Dumb Friends League)—a shelter whose legacy I deeply admired. My partner and I moved to Denver, and I started a new chapter.

The organization's scale was staggering, with over 300 employees. Managing two departments in that environment was both humbling and exciting. A turning point came during a 1:1 meeting with a colleague in the behavior department, a dear friend who had been on the team for a decade. We had finished our agenda but still had time, so I asked, *"I've been managing this team for a few months now, but you've been here for years. Do you have any advice for me?"*

He didn't hesitate: *"I think you might be trying too hard to please everyone. And when you do that, people end up getting less from you. You can't always split the baby, so to speak, but you can focus on making the right decisions and being there for them, regardless of how they feel about it."*

Cringe-worthy metaphor aside, it was exactly what I needed to hear. That advice helped me step more fully into leadership and into my next role.

Leading without People-Pleasing

In 2022, a director-level position became available, overseeing my existing teams and the veterinary services and foster departments. I applied, interviewed, and got the job. Now, I've been "Directoring" (yes, I might have made that word up) since 2022, with five managers reporting to me and 75 indirect reports across the organization.

At this level, there's no room for people-pleasing—only radical candor. I believe my willingness to learn from those I lead, my care for my teams, my commitment to healthy boundaries, and my humility have kept me grounded.

Every day, I remain open to advice, to learn from mistakes, and to grow from every interaction with staff members, volunteers, patrons, and community partners.

If I could offer advice to others stepping into, or already in, animal welfare leadership, it would be this: Work hard but also take care of yourself. Lead bravely, stay humble, and keep learning. Love animals, but don't forget to love people, too. Yes, they may sometimes be part of the problem, but they are always part of the solution.

***Jes Cytron** is an animal welfare leader with more than a decade of experience in both limited- and open-admission shelters. Starting as a kennel technician in 2013, Cytron worked their way up through nearly every role in animal care, adoptions, foster management, and shelter operations before moving into senior leadership. Formerly serving as Director of Shelter Behavior and Veterinary Services at Humane Colorado (formerly Dumb Friends League) in Denver, Colorado, Cytron oversaw five managers and 75 team members, guiding programs for behavior, veterinary services, transfer, and foster care. She is currently the Director of Shelter Operations at the East Bay SPCA in Oakland, California, where she oversees six departments and leads programming for public-facing and shelter-focused behavior, medical, adoption, and intake services across two facilities that support the people and animals of the Bay Area.*

Cytron is known for their expertise in pathway planning for behaviorally complex shelter animals, their commitment to healthy leadership practices, and their belief that animal welfare is as much about supporting people as it is about saving pets. A Certified Animal Welfare Administrator since 2023, Cytron approaches leadership with curiosity, humility, and radical candor.

Outside of work, they enjoy cooking competition shows, arts and crafts, and relaxing with their partner and as many chihuahuas and pit bulls as possible. They currently have one of each at home and foster many others.

"If you can't influence others, you're not a leader—you're just a manager."

Denise Deisler

The Words are Not the Fight. The Animals Are.

My career began in the Air Force, which I had loved, but I was medically separated after an injury. Returning to school and entering the nonprofit sector gave me a new purpose. At United Way, I enjoyed the fast-paced, do-it-all environment, but one thing became clear: most nonprofits were caught in a cycle of doing. Few had strategic plans to address the issues they were facing.

I was working in a freelance PR role at United Way in Richmond, Virginia, when a friend called and said, "Something exciting is happening at the SPCA. You should come talk to the executive director." I thought animal shelters were full of nice people who just loved pets. I didn't realize animal welfare was a professional field.

I also didn't know how broken the system was—or how many animals were dying simply because there was no plan to save them. But when I met with the team at the Richmond SPCA, I saw something radically different: a board of directors who had spent a year studying best practices across the country. They were inspired by San Francisco's no-kill movement and committed to doing better. They didn't have it all figured out yet. But they knew they needed to try. That was enough for me. They were looking for a communications person, and I signed on.

Wearing Every Hat

Not long after I started, someone in operations left unexpectedly. I raised my hand and said, "I can learn that job." Then someone in human resources left, and I said, "I can do that too." Then finance. Same thing. Again and again, I raised my hand, not because I had the answers or experience, but because I was willing to learn. Like so many of us in the field, I wore many hats because the need was so great.

There were no manuals. No formal training. But it was a small team, and we had big goals. I had to teach myself what I didn't know—and fast. It was a crash course in sheltering, fundraising, and leadership. But it was also thrilling. We weren't just managing animals. We were saving lives and transforming a community.

When I started, we had 13 staff in a cramped, outdated building. When I left as Chief Operating Officer, we had built a 64,000-square-foot facility, expanded to 80 employees, and created a national model for change. We proved that when you pair vision with a solid plan, you can move mountains.

On the Road Again

After Richmond, I spent 18 months consulting. I worked with shelters across the country, helping them replicate the change we had created in Virginia. It was satisfying work, but when one of my clients in Florida asked me to stay on as their CEO, I said yes.

That's when I joined the Humane Society of Manatee County in Bradenton, Florida. They were ready for a transformation, and I was excited to be a part of the team.

During my tenure, we helped the city to pass a no-kill resolution. We engaged the public in new ways and challenged our own assumptions about what was possible. I was a staunch no-kill advocate but let me be clear: the words didn't matter to me. It was all about saving lives. And, we were successful in Manatee not because we clung to a label, but because we listened to the community, worked in partnership, and stayed focused on the goal: saving lives.

A Full Circle Moment

Years earlier, while I was still in Richmond, Virginia, leaders from Jacksonville, Florida, had toured our facility. They were inspired by what we were doing, and we agreed to become sister cities. I traveled there regularly, offering advice and support.

Then, years later, after their shelter suffered a devastating fire and progress had stalled, they reached out to me again. They needed someone to finish what we had started together. I didn't want to leave the Humane Society of Manatee County, but it felt like a full-circle moment—a chance to finish some of what I had started with my consulting work. I accepted the position.

What I found upon arrival was challenging. The organization had pulled back from taking in strays, and intake had plummeted from 13,000 to 3,000 animals. But that didn't mean there were fewer animals. It just meant they were going to the municipal shelter, which was overwhelmed. We were still working out of trailers and makeshift offices. There were plastic bags over the computers in case it rained. With new energy and focus, though, our intake and adoptions climbed to 8,000 annually. I was amazed. That grit and commitment became the foundation for everything that came next.

Building with a Purpose

It was clear we needed a real shelter. The trailers were falling apart, and staff was working in conditions that weren't safe or sustainable. So, we launched a $15 million capital campaign.

Fundraising at that scale is never easy. But we were strategic. We didn't want to risk the operational dollars we already had, so we focused on engaging new donors—particularly major philanthropists who had never previously supported animal welfare. We presented them with data, a clear plan, and proof that our model was effective. And they responded.

Petco Love stepped up with a significant grant. Others followed. We ended up receiving multiple gifts worth over $1 million, as well as many more in the six-figure range. When the building was complete, we had zero debt. We built a place people wanted to come to, a space that welcomed adopters, made staff proud, and gave animals the care they deserved.

Leadership in a Crisis

Then came COVID. The first thing I did was gather the team and say, *"We're going to get through this safely. And no one is going to lose their job."*

People needed reassurance. They needed stability. And they needed a leader who wasn't afraid to act. We never stopped serving. We just did it differently. Adoptions continued. Spay/neuter continued. The pet food bank continued.

We followed the science behind COVID, but we didn't fall into groupthink. We made our own decisions based on our own community. We implemented social distancing measures, staggered shifts, and mandatory COVID-19 testing. We had backup plans and contingency models in place. We communicated constantly—internally and externally. And we got through it.

What I Know Now

Looking back, there are a dozen things I wish I had known when I started. But here are the most important:

→ **Leadership is influence.** If you can't inspire people to follow you, you're not leading. You're managing.

→ **Be flexible.** Leadership is situational. What worked yesterday may not work tomorrow. You must be the leader your organization needs in that moment.

→ **Know yourself.** Understand your limitations. Build a team that complements your gaps. And listen to the people who will tell you the truth.

→ **Know your community.** Don't copy/paste from other organizations. Take inspiration from others, but build your model around your local reality.

→ **Don't mistake patience for inaction.** I used to say, *"Patience equals dead dogs and cats."* That was a limited belief. Now I understand that patience, when paired with perspective, is powerful. It helps you move mountains in the right direction.

We don't do this work for the accolades. We do it for the lives we save. But I'll admit: being recognized with a Lifetime Achievement Award by Best Friends Animal Society was deeply meaningful. It made me pause and reflect on the decades of learning, adapting, struggling, and leading.

This field isn't easy. But when you lead with purpose, stay grounded in community, and never stop learning, you can help shape a future where no healthy or treatable animal dies simply because they are homeless. That's why I stayed. That's why I raised my hand again and again.

Because the words aren't the fight. The animals are.

***Denise Deisler** has spent her career transforming communities through lifesaving animal welfare work. She joined the Jacksonville Humane Society (JHS) in 2011, where, as CEO, she immediately forged key partnerships, increased revenue while reducing expenses, and launched innovative programs, including a kitten nursery, a community resource center, and a renewed focus on shelter transfers. These initiatives saved more than 1,000 additional lives in her first year alone. Under her leadership, Jacksonville became one of the largest U.S. cities to achieve a 90+% live release rate, sustaining that milestone for five of the last six years.*

Deisler also led the $15 million campaign to rebuild JHS after a devastating 2007 fire, overseeing the design and construction of a new 44,000-square-foot shelter that opened in November 2017. Beyond Jacksonville, she founded Florida Leaders in Lifesaving, an inclusive coalition dedicated to increasing lifesaving across the state.

Her earlier leadership roles include serving as Executive Director of the Humane Society of Manatee County, where she helped end trap-and-kill policies for community cats and guided the county toward a no-kill plan, and as Chief Operating Officer of the Richmond SPCA in Richmond, Virginia, where she played a key role in transforming Richmond's approach to animal homelessness.

Recognized nationally for her leadership, Deisler was named a Maddie's Fund Hero in 2018, received the Best Friends Animal Society National Advancement Award in 2019, and the Best Friends Lifetime Achievement Award in 2025. She serves on leadership committees for organizations including Petco Love, Purina, Best Friends Animal Society, and American Pets Alive. A sought-after trainer and consultant, she shares her expertise on no-kill strategies, board development, and community engagement nationwide.

Deisler lives with her husband, Bernie, her granddaughter Emma, their dogs, Yogi and Shelli, and their cat, Purrl.

"True leadership means spotting an opportunity others might overlook—and having the persistence to turn it into lasting impact."

Susana Della Maddalena

Following Your Gut: Embracing New Ideas That Change Things for Animals

Great leaders know that innovation often starts by questioning the status quo. Sometimes, the best solutions come from reimagining what seems routine—and sometimes, from listening closely to your team and empowering them to bring bold ideas forward. I have been fortunate to experience this firsthand throughout my career, watching creative ideas turn into transformative change. Here are a few of them.

A Far-Out Idea at the Checkout

When I joined PetSmart Charities as Executive Director in 2003, we were generating about $8 million annually through two promotions, an in-store campaign called *"Just a Buck, Change Their Luck,"* and a companywide payroll deduction program.

One of the biggest challenges with the in-store campaign was that it relied on cashiers asking customers for donations, creating an awkward situation for both the employees, who were often uncomfortable asking, and the customers, who didn't always want to be put on the spot.

I wondered if there was a different way. What if we programmed the Point-of-Sale system to automatically prompt customers for a donation at checkout? No more inconsistent cashier compliance, no more awkwardness—just a consistent, respectful way to invite every customer to give.

It was a far-out idea at the time, but after building the case, PetSmart's Chief Operating Officer authorized me to work with IT to make it happen. Six months later, we rolled it out across 1,600 stores. In one year, our income grew from $8 million to $18 million. A decade later, donations had climbed to $45 million.

We were the first retailer to deploy this kind of automated fundraising prompt, and it transformed PetSmart Charities' ability to help homeless pets in a meaningful way. That system is still in use today, enabling shelters across the country to receive critical funding for their programs.

But my greatest reward wasn't just the pin pad. It was the opportunity to listen to and support my team as they brought forth other bold ideas that would change the field forever.

Scaling Up a Game-Changing Clinic Model

Shortly after I started at PetSmart Charities, our Director of Grants brought me a proposal from a small spay/neuter clinic in North Carolina working out of a converted bank building. They were performing thousands of surgeries safely in that tiny space.

Being new to the field, I asked her to walk me through why she thought it was special. She explained the critical role of spay/neuter in reducing shelter intake and how this model—high-volume, high-quality, efficient surgeries—could be a game changer.

At a conference a month later, we met with the clinic's Executive and Medical Directors. Within minutes, it was clear they were on to something revolutionary. The question was whether it could scale nationally.

In 2004, we approved the proposal, beginning a long and fruitful partnership with Humane Alliance, now known as The ASPCA Spay/Neuter Alliance. With our funding and that of other partners, Humane Alliance grew into a national training center in Asheville, North Carolina, and built a network of high-volume, high-quality spay/neuter clinics across the country.

They helped transform the paradigm, making pediatric spay/neuter standard practice in animal welfare. By the time I left, PetSmart Charities was funding approximately $10 million annually in spay/neuter grants, preventing the birth of countless unwanted litters.

Professionalizing Transport to Save More Lives

Another moment of listening came when my team urged me to professionalize transport. My predecessor had started exploring relocation, recognizing that dogs and puppies were dying in under-resourced shelters even though they could easily be adopted in other communities. Transport was already happening, but often in sporadic and unsafe ways.

Over the next year, we developed and launched Rescue Waggin', a national best-in-class transport program. The idea was simple: relocate dogs to shelters with adopters and resources, while at the same time providing grants to the source shelters so they could eventually build their own capacity.

One email I received still gives me goosebumps. A small southern shelter, located by a dump with open-air kennels, had never named their dogs because nearly all were euthanized. On the morning of their first transport, the director wrote: "The sun came up over our shelter as we boarded 15 dogs onto the Rescue Waggin', bound for new homes. I wiped away tears as I said goodbye to Helen Reddy, Oreo, and the others—dogs who were leaving our shelter not in green garbage bags, but on their way to loving homes."

By 2013, Rescue Waggin' had transported nearly 100,000 dogs and helped hundreds of shelters save more lives.

Creating Space for Others

Yes, my 15 minutes of fame may have been launching the in-store pin pad donation, but the real achievement was building and fostering a team of passionate professionals who together launched programs that changed the landscape of animal welfare. Humane Alliance, Rescue Waggin', and many other initiatives proved that when leaders listen, empower, and follow through, far-out ideas become lifesaving realities.

True leadership means spotting an opportunity others might overlook—and having the persistence to turn it into lasting impact.

Susana (Sue) Della Maddalena, MBA, *has dedicated her career to building partnerships, programs, and organizations that change the lives of animals and the people who care for them. Currently serving as Senior Advisor, Strategic Partnerships for Best Friends Animal Society, Della Maddalena draws on decades of leadership experience in animal welfare, including ten years as Executive Director of PetSmart Charities.*

During her time at PetSmart Charities, Della Maddalena oversaw transformative growth in the organization's fundraising and grantmaking capacity, helping to expand programs that funded shelters, spay/neuter initiatives, and adoption events nationwide. She later served as CEO and President of Central Oklahoma Humane Society in Oklahoma City, Oklahoma, and as Executive Director of Altered Tails, a high-volume spay/neuter organization in Arizona that significantly reduced shelter intake and euthanasia rates in Maricopa County.

Della Maddalena is also a cancer survivor whose personal resilience has deepened her understanding of perseverance, empathy, and the value of creating lasting impact. She holds a Master of Business Administration degree from Thunderbird School of Global Management and brings a strategic, results-driven approach to every role she undertakes.

Whether guiding national initiatives or strengthening local programs, Della Maddalena's leadership is defined by her ability to see possibilities others might overlook—and to inspire teams, partners, and communities to work together for the animals who need them most.

"Leadership isn't about waiting until you're ready. It's about recognizing an opportunity and having the nerve to jump in."

Rick DuCharme

I Didn't Plan to Start a Nonprofit. Here's What Happened When I Did.

My journey into animal welfare didn't begin in a shelter or veterinary clinic. It started on a neighborhood street—with a stray dog and a lesson from my mother. I was about ten years old, during a time when kids left the house at sunrise and came home when the streetlights flickered on. Every time I saw a loose dog, I brought it home, hoping to help. My mom would do her best to find the owner.

But one day, after another unsuccessful search, she looked at me and said, *"Rick, sometimes it might be better to leave them where you find them. They might find their way home. If we take them to the shelter, they could be euthanized."*

That moment stuck with me. Even as a kid, I understood the weight of her words. I stopped bringing dogs home, but I never forgot that lesson. It planted the seed for a lifelong commitment to finding a better way.

From Product Pitches to Animal Advocacy

I started my career in business—working in equipment manufacturing and climbing the corporate ladder. But animal welfare was never far from my mind. I donated to Best Friends Animal Society, followed the no-kill movement, and read everything I could about targeted spay/neuter and TNR (trap-neuter-return) programs.

Then one day, I read an article in the Jacksonville newspaper: the mayor was forming a task force to improve animal services. I applied, eager to offer what I had learned.

At the first meeting, I didn't show up empty-handed. I brought 12 binders, one for each task force member, filled with research and data on progressive strategies. That gesture earned me the role of subcommittee chair for policies, procedures, and protocols. I used that platform to emphasize the importance of targeted spay/neuter programs in every meeting.

Eventually, we submitted a 17-page report to the mayor with bold recommendations, including TNR, high-volume spay/neuter, and the construction of a new shelter. The task force disbanded, and I waited to see what would come of it.

An Accidental Founder

Soon after, the mayor's office called. They wanted to launch a city-wide spay/neuter initiative and suggested I start a nonprofit to lead it.

I didn't want to start a nonprofit. I offered to help existing organizations apply for the contract, but no one stepped forward. I felt like I had no choice. If things were going to move forward, I would have to launch the nonprofit myself. So I did; right there at my kitchen table, filling out the paperwork for what would become First Coast No More Homeless Pets. Best Friends Animal Society allowed me to use the "No More Homeless Pets" name, and with support from Peter Marsh and Esther Meckler, our first two board members, we launched the organization.

Even before our 501(c)(3) status was approved, the city awarded us a $300,000 contract to run a targeted spay/neuter program. We launched a voucher system with around 20 participating veterinary clinics. Clients paid a small co-pay that covered a rabies vaccine, sterilization, and a city license tag.

Scaling Up with Purpose

As the economy improved, however, fewer private vets wanted to participate. So, we opened our own clinic, a 600-square-foot converted grooming salon. The space was so small we had to check clients in under a tent outside. Over the years, we eventually expanded to 2,200 square feet, and then to more than 20,000 square feet of medical space, with another 8,000 square feet for administration and 8,000 square feet of warehouse space.

By the time I stepped down in 2019, we had 125 employees, including 25 veterinarians, served 65,000 patients annually, and performed over 22,000 spay/neuter surgeries each year.

What made us different? We scaled everything to meet the need. Our pet food bank wasn't a few bags on a shelf. We had forklifts and pallet racks. When a man brought in a sick dog during a vaccine clinic saying he couldn't afford a full-service vet, we helped him. That encounter changed my thinking. Spay/neuter is vital, but pets get sick more than once in their lifetimes lifetime. We needed to do more.

What I've Learned

Back then, there was no textbook on how to do this—and we didn't have the internet or social media to guide us. Most of us were learning as we went. I didn't follow a leadership playbook; I figured things out through trial and error, trusted good people, and made decisions based on what felt right for the mission. Over time, a few core lessons emerged that shaped how I led, and how we grew.

1. Hire people smarter than you. I didn't build this alone. In the early days, a woman named Faith Martin offered to help with accounting as a volunteer. When the city announced an audit, I called her, and she organized 20 boxes of records and helped us pass it. Then came Debbie Fields. She walked into an adoption event and asked if we needed help. She soon became our volunteer coordinator, marketing director, and eventually president. I always sought out the best people—those with skills I didn't have—and then gave them the tools, trust, and support to thrive. Whether paid or volunteer, a well-supported team will give you their best.

2. Say "yes" before you're ready. One of our biggest turning points came when the city offered to send us all the feral cats from the city shelter—about 5,000 a year—to spay, vaccinate, ear-tip, and return. I said "*yes*" without knowing how we would pay for it. Best

Friends Animal Society stepped in with a grant, and that Shelter-Neuter-Return (SNR) program became a game-changer. It was likely the first program of its kind in the country and helped establish an entirely new category of lifesaving work—now practiced by shelters nationwide. It taught me that leadership means saying *"yes"* when the moment calls for it—and figuring out how you will do it along the way.

3. Know you'll evolve as a leader. In the beginning, I thought I had all the answers. If you weren't saving 90%, doing TNR, or fully on board, you weren't doing enough. But I've learned to appreciate the gray areas in our work. Communities are different. Strategies evolve. Sometimes the best leadership move is to listen, adapt, and respect that others may be walking a different, but equally valuable path. Still, I don't regret that early drive. That boldness helped us take on big challenges. It got things done.

4. Don't assume the experts have it all figured out. Early on, it's easy to believe the big names in animal welfare hold all the answers. But the truth is, we're all learning. What worked five years ago might not work now. Study what others have done, but don't let their roadmaps limit your vision. Our most impactful programs weren't copied from someone else. They were built from listening to our community, identifying gaps, and trying something new.

5. Mega-size the mission. If the problem is big, your response has to be bigger. When we started, over 36,000 pets were entering Jacksonville shelters each year, and more than 26,000 were dying there. We couldn't make a dent with small efforts. That's why we built large-scale infrastructure, like clinics, food banks, and adoption events. We didn't do anything small because the need wasn't small. Over time, those large-scale efforts dramatically reduced intake and brought shelter euthanasia down to fewer than 1,000 animals a year.

If there's one thread running through all of this, it's that leadership isn't about having a perfect plan. It's about showing up with conviction. It's recognizing when something needs to be done, and being willing to take the first step, even if you're not sure how you'll take the second. That's how change starts. That's how progress is made. And when you build something that truly matters, people will show up to help build it with you.

***Rick DuCharme** is a nationally recognized leader in animal welfare, known for bringing business discipline and bold vision to lifesaving work. After a career in the heavy equipment industry, DuCharme channeled his skills and passion into volunteering on the Mayor's Task Force for Animal Control in Jacksonville, Florida. There, he became a driving force in the city's transformation to one of the nation's first large no-kill communities.*

In 2002, DuCharme founded First Coast No More Homeless Pets (FCNMHP) in Jacksonville, Florida, a nonprofit dedicated to ending the killing of dogs and cats in Duval County and beyond. As CEO, he grew FCNMHP into a $10+ million organization serving a 10,000-square-mile area across two states. The organization operated two large safety-net hospitals, employing more than 165 staff (including 20+ veterinarians) and performing over 22,000 targeted spay/neuter surgeries annually. DuCharme ensured targeted spay/neuter remained a priority, while also expanding into a regional pet food bank, and launching SNR programs and Mega Adoption Events. These efforts, particularly his pioneering Feral Freedom shelter-based TNR program, reduced shelter intake by more than 50% and feline euthanasia to record lows, inspiring similar models nationwide.

DuCharme also co-founded Target Zero, helping dozens of communities increase their live-release rates, and Community Cat Clinics in metro Atlanta, Georgia, offering, offering affordable feline care to expand access to services.

Today, through RLD Consulting Services, DuCharme works with animal welfare organizations, veterinary clinics, and mission-driven for-profits across the country to expand access to care, launch and scale spay/neuter programs, and build sustainable operations. His consulting specialties include feasibility studies, strategic planning, implementation, and sustainability.

From building mega-adoption events to designing community cat programs now replicated nationwide, DuCharme's career reflects a single, unwavering mission: to create practical, scalable solutions that save more animals' lives.

Adopt
me!

"When precious lives hang in the balance, good is not good enough."

Ed Duvin

Words and Deeds: A Leader's Call to Master History, Management, and Moral Courage

Leadership in the humane movement is not a single talent or technique, but a careful blending of skills, ethics, and vision. It requires looking backward and forward at the same time: backward to understand the struggles, triumphs, and mistakes of those who came before us, and forward to chart a deliberate path toward a better future for those we serve. Without the wisdom of history, we risk walking in circles, repeating patterns that have already led to setbacks or stagnation. Without strong management, that wisdom never takes shape in the real world. And without ethics at the core, all the skill and planning in the world amount to little.

Learning from History

Learning the movement's history is a good starting place, as those who came before us paved the path we now travel. It provides us with a road map, illuminating promising directions as well as dead ends and detours. History is there for learning, but only if we avail ourselves of its wisdom.

The adage that those who ignore history are doomed to repeat it holds true for movements. The challenge is not learning isolated facts about our past, but understanding the dynamics of social change from a historical perspective.

In this regard, there is no better resource than the work of the late Bill Moyer. He was an activist and educator who researched the history of social movements, developing the Movement Action Plan (MAP). The following passage from Moyer, written in 1987, underscores how essential historical patterns are to social change:

"Within a few years after achieving the goals of 'take-off,' every major social movement of the past twenty years has undergone a significant collapse, in which activists believed that their movements had failed, the power institutions were too powerful, and their own efforts were futile."

This is hardly an inspiring depiction of social movements. If we are to avoid a similar fate going forward, understanding the rhythms of history as applied to social change is our best teacher.

The Eight Stages of the Movement Action Plan (MAP)

For leaders seeking to anticipate challenges and sustain momentum, here is what Moyer's MAP identifies as the eight stages that most movements experience. These are not meant to be rigid rules, but a tool to help leaders anticipate challenges, recognize progress, and navigate discouragement.

1. Normal Times—The issue exists, but the public and institutions pay little attention. Activists work quietly, building networks and gathering information.

2. Prove the Failure of Official Institutions—Activists reveal that existing systems are either unwilling or unable to address the problem, thereby helping to shift public perception.

3. Ripening Conditions—Awareness and concern grow. Small groups begin organizing, and the groundwork is laid for wider action.

4. Take-Off—A triggering event or breakthrough moment propels the movement into the public eye, sparking rapid growth in activism and attention.

5. Perception of Failure—Momentum slows. The public's attention shifts, activists burn out, and many fear the movement has failed despite real gains.

6. Majority Public Opinion—Through steady work, the movement's core messages take root in mainstream culture, and a majority begins to support the cause.

7. Success—Policy changes, institutional reforms, or cultural shifts reflect the movement's goals, though these victories often require continued vigilance.

8. Continuing the Struggle—The work is not over. Leaders consolidate gains, address new challenges, and work to prevent backsliding.

The MAP Framework wasn't intended to be a rigid template, but rather a tool to better understand and surmount societal resistance to change. By recognizing the stage a movement is in, leaders can avoid common pitfalls, such as mistaking the "perception of failure" for actual failure, and make better strategic choices.

In the animal welfare field, these stages are visible everywhere if we take the time to look. The push for spay/neuter, once ignored (*Normal Times*), gained attention after studies proved that traditional sheltering failed to stem overpopulation (*Prove the Failure*). Public campaigns and grassroots groups built awareness (*Ripening Conditions*), leading to surges in surgeries and legislation (*Take-Off*). Later, frustration grew when euthanasia numbers didn't drop as quickly as hoped (*Perception of Failure*), but sustained education and outreach shifted the majority public opinion toward sterilization and adoption (*Majority Public Opinion*). Each accomplishment (Success), from puppy mill bans to trap-neuter-return policies, reminds us that our work continues (*Continuing the Struggle*).

When we see our work through this lens, it becomes clear that we're part of a larger historical arc, not just isolated campaigns. And if we are to move that arc forward, leaders in animal welfare must develop the skills to recognize these patterns, respond strategically, and guide their organizations through each stage.

As a leader, your ability to translate these lessons into action will define the true impact of your work.

From History to Management

History offers us the lessons; management determines whether we apply them effectively. If you are stepping into this role, understand that you carry both the privilege and the weight of that responsibility.

Moving to another pivotal dimension of leadership, good intentions rarely produce results without highly proficient management. Malpractice is usually associated with the medical profession, but it also applies to altruistic endeavors that fail to honor their mission. In effect, we hang out our "shingle" as protectors of other beings, thereby assuming the concomitant responsibilities inherent in that commitment.

In the profit sector, the bottom line drives the quest for excellence. For us, our animal family represents the "bottom line," but we lack the necessary emphasis on performance standards. Some organizations place the three Ms—money, membership, and media—at the forefront, but organizational excellence is best measured by meaningful results.

Strategic Planning and Performance Standards

There are many ingredients involved in establishing demanding performance standards, with strategic planning serving as an optimal starting point. Distilled to its essence, a strategic plan is a clear vision of where an organization is headed and the best approach to achieve its goals. It requires revisiting and, when necessary, revising the mission statement, followed by charting a course to meet defined goals through planned implementation phases.

For a potential leader, mastering this process is not optional. It is the foundation on which every program and initiative will stand.

Programs are then formulated to transform the vision into reality, with diligent monitoring to ensure that objectives are met on a timely basis. Sound programming should be developed in a complementary manner, as each element of the operational structure should support the others, much like spokes maintaining the integrity of a wheel. This integrated approach not only increases productivity but also provides organizational cohesion.

The Moral Compass of Leadership

Even the most skilled management is hollow without a moral compass to guide it. For you as a leader, that compass must be unwavering, especially when the easier path may tempt you away from your values.

Although striving for managerial excellence is vital, it has little meaning if not accompanied by unswerving ethical principles. In over a half-century of consulting for several social causes, only a few organizations prioritized the need for a sound ethical foundation. Martin Luther King spoke of the need to align words with deeds, and moral consistency demands that we meet that standard.

Ethical precepts should not be viewed in a vacuum, but rather as an integral component of our core values. If nonhumans are ever to gain the moral and legal standing they deserve, we need to live the values we ask the public to embrace. Otherwise, we not only fail other beings, but ourselves.

Final Thoughts

In conclusion, it's clearly unrealistic and self-righteous to expect everyone to be proficient at management and paragons of virtue. However, we must continue to master our craft, as we are the last line of defense for those we serve.

Choosing this path requires commitment to constant growth. The animals and people who depend on you deserve nothing less.

When precious lives hang in the balance, good is not good enough.

***Ed Duvin**, retired publisher, nonprofit leader, and foundational influencer of the no-kill movement, is perhaps best known for his role as the publisher of Animalines, an influential newsletter that ran from 1987 to 1991 and became a platform for bold, thought-provoking commentary on animal welfare. His groundbreaking 1989 essay "In the Name of Mercy" challenged the field to rethink its reliance on euthanasia in shelters, urging outcome-based approaches,* *community education, and a full commitment to the lives of companion animals. The essay sparked national discussion and influenced a generation of leaders, advocates, and policymakers.*

Over a four-decade career, Duvin consulted for numerous social justice organizations, bringing the same blend of ethical vision and strategic discipline that defined his animal welfare work. He served as associate director of In Defense of Animals and as Executive Director of both the Center for Respect of Life and Environment and Building Caring Communities. Duvin also founded Project ZERO and Walking the Walk initiatives dedicated to raising ethical, strategic, and managerial standards in the humane community. He has worked with national and international organizations, mentored emerging leaders, and contributed extensively to dialogue on how movements evolve and succeed.

Duvin's broader writing, most notably "Speciesism: Alive and Well" (1990), pressed the movement toward measurable results, rigorous performance standards, and uncompromising moral clarity. His essays are frequently cited by advocates and historians of the no-kill era, and his later reflections connect civil rights and anti-poverty advocacy to animal protection, underscoring a lifelong concern for justice and organizational excellence.

Today, Duvin's work remains a touchstone for leaders seeking to align history, management discipline, and ethical purpose, the triad many credit with moving shelters toward humane, data-driven systems that save lives.

"Scarcity had become a mindset, not a reality... That shift—from scarcity to possibility—isn't about wishful thinking. It's about helping others see that the door is already open."

20

Tracy Elliott

What It Takes to Stay the Course in Nonprofit Work

I didn't begin my career in animal welfare. I came to it later, after working in education, banking, and HIV/AIDS advocacy. But when I entered this field, something felt profoundly different. It wasn't just about the animals; it was the people. There's a generosity in animal welfare I had never experienced anywhere else. People pick up the phone to talk to each other. They share what they have learned. They support each other across organizations, across geographies, without hesitation or ego.

And it made me want to do the same.

Since then, I have led nonprofits on the verge of collapse, rebuilt cultures, mentored emerging leaders, and helped staff rediscover their passion and drive. I have also had a front-row seat to some of the sector's deepest challenges, particularly in terms of how we lead, whom we listen to, and what gets in the way of progress.

The Leadership Style That's Served Me Best

Over the years, my approach to leadership has evolved into *supportive, humane leadership*. It's not top-down. It's not command-and-control. It's about giving people the tools, agency, and encouragement they need to thrive.

I believe in setting a clear vision and aligning people around it. I bring others into strategy conversations, not just for buy-in, but because collective thinking builds better outcomes. I don't micromanage. If I have a flaw, it's probably that I trust too much. However, I would rather place my confidence in people and risk being let down than try to control them into compliance.

And here's what I have found: *when you trust people, most rise to the occasion*.

However, even the most intentional leadership can be hindered by the structures surrounding it. In the nonprofit world, one of the most influential, and often most complex, of these structures is the board.

Boards: The Missing Link — or Roadblock

I have served on more than 20 nonprofit boards and reported to several more. And here's the truth that most leaders whisper behind closed doors: *Our governance system is broken. It's outdated, inconsistent, and often lacks the checks, balances, and support that leaders need to succeed.*

In most cases, one-third of a board is engaged and effective. One-third is waiting to be told what to do. And one-third is disengaged entirely. The result is groupthink—social norms that discourage healthy dissent and lead to too many decisions being driven by the loudest voice in the room.

When that happens, the board stops being a compass and becomes a constraint.

I have walked into board meetings unsure whether I would still have a job when I walked out—and I know I'm not alone in that. It's a deeply stressful reality that few outside the role understand.

Boards don't need to manage staff. They need to support leadership, hold themselves accountable, and stay focused on the mission. That means understanding the difference between oversight and overreach. It means asking better questions, not just giving more opinions. It means recognizing that their most important role is to build trust, ensure alignment with strategic goals, and help sustain long-term impact, rather than reacting to short-term noise.

The best board members I have worked with do a few simple but powerful things. They read the materials in advance. They show up prepared. They listen before they speak. They create space for new voices, ask questions with curiosity (not judgment), and resist the urge to lead from the sidelines. They understand that being a good board member isn't about having the final word; it's about fostering the right environment for leadership to succeed. That kind of support matters, especially in a field where the stakes are high and the weight feels personal.

So, How Do We Stay in the Work — and Stay Well?

In a field as heart-centered and resource-constrained as ours, burnout isn't just common, it's a reality. But it doesn't have to be inevitable. After decades of leadership, here are the three lessons I return to again and again:

1. Be Brutally Honest with Yourself. Leadership requires courage, and that starts with looking in the mirror and asking the hard questions: *Am I still the right person for this role? Am I leading from a place of strength or from a place of survival? Am I staying because I feel guilty... or because I still have something to give?*

I once asked a burned-out operations leader, *"Do you need permission to leave?"* She sighed and said, *"That's exactly what I need."*

Sometimes we hold on out of guilt, afraid that walking away means abandoning the mission. But knowing when to go is as vital as knowing when to step up. We need to normalize that truth, especially in our field.

2. Let Go of the Scarcity Mindset. Nonprofits live in a culture of scarcity: *"We don't have enough." "We can't afford it." "No one will donate again."*

But leading from fear keeps organizations stuck.

Scarcity thinking doesn't just affect morale; it affects cognition. When we fixate on what we lack, our executive functioning suffers. We make poorer decisions. We lose creativity. And we spread that anxiety to our teams.

I have seen it firsthand. At one organization, staff had to request permission to purchase notepads, even though they had substantial funds in the bank. Scarcity had become a mindset, not a reality.

That's why I tell leaders there is enough out there for us to run our organizations: enough money, enough donors, enough adopters.

But we have to believe it, act accordingly, and align our mission, message, and methods with confidence. Not panic.

3. Lead Others into Abundance

It's not enough to shift your own mindset. As leaders, we must bring others along with us. Creating a culture of abundance begins with how we communicate, plan, and lead.

Sometimes that means encouraging initiative instead of waiting for permission. Sometimes it means challenging assumptions, like the idea that a donor won't give again or that a team can't handle a stretch goal. More than anything, it means modeling what's possible instead of reinforcing what's not.

I once had a board chair say, *"We can't ask that donor again for a donation."* I responded, *"Let's not decide for them."* I picked up the phone, thanked the donor for their past generosity, and asked if they would consider making the gift again. *"Sure, happy to,"* they said.

We didn't have to overthink it. We just had to ask.

That shift—from scarcity to possibility—isn't about wishful thinking. It's about helping others see that the door is already open, and support is waiting to come through.

Final Thoughts

I have worked in large cities and rural communities, led established institutions and organizations on the edge. I have taught, mentored, fundraised, and rebuilt. And through it all, one thing has remained true: leadership isn't about having all the answers. It's about showing up with clarity, humility, and heart—even when the path ahead is uncertain. And it's about staying open to answers, wherever they may come from.

Animal welfare is a field of deep compassion and grit. It demands that we care fiercely while navigating systems that often do not support us. But, it also calls on us to lead differently, building healthier cultures, challenging old assumptions, and helping others believe in what's possible again.

I don't have it all figured out, but I've lived the questions and stayed in the work. I've led through uncertainty, spoken up when it mattered, and done my best to bring others with me. Because leadership, at its core, is about making room—for people, for progress, for ideas—so what's next has space to grow.

That's how change happens: not all at once, but because someone chose to stay and keep building.

Tracy Elliott, *Executive Director of the Asheville Humane Society in Asheville, North Carolina, has dedicated more than four decades to the Social Sector, including 22 years as a nonprofit CEO. His leadership journey has spanned education, banking, HIV/AIDS services, youth development, and animal welfare—guided by a personal mission that views the Social Sector as the "privilege of serving others" through cooperative action to solve the world's problems, our country's challenges, and our communities' needs.*

Elliott earned his Bachelor of Arts from Harvard University and his Master of Nonprofit Administration, magna cum laude, from the University of Notre Dame's Mendoza College of Business. He has since led organizations through crisis and transformation, earning recognition for building cultures of humane leadership, strengthening organizational systems, and advancing missions with urgency. His CEO roles have included The Anti-Cruelty Society in Chicago, Illinois, AID Atlanta in Atlanta, Georgia, and College Mentors for Kids and The Damien Center, both in Indianapolis, Indiana.

Through his practice, T. Elliott Social Impact, he mentors leaders and boards across the country, helping them optimize their impact, align people with purpose, and adopt an abundance mindset.

Elliott's leadership has been recognized by governors, national organizations, and community groups alike. Honors include the Sagamore of the Wabash Award, Indiana's highest honor for exceptional contributions to one's fellow citizens, and numerous community leadership awards, including 50 Top LGBTQIA+ Leaders in Atlanta by Phoenix Magazine, Building Bridges of Understanding Award by the Indianapolis Men's Chorus, and the Distinguished Service Award from the Emmett Till Foundation in Chicago.

Throughout his career, Elliott has sought to banish scarcity thinking, inspire collaboration, and prepare organizations to thrive. Today, at Asheville Humane Society and beyond, he continues to champion humane leadership and organizational vitality.

"If you leave and everything collapses, you weren't really leading. You were just holding it together with your own two hands."

21

Joe Elmore

Building a Resilient Team That Can Weather Any Storm

When I first started at Charleston Animal Society in Charleston, South Carolina, the challenges were visible on every face. The organization had a history, but also faced strain—financial pressures, morale issues, and the unspoken question of whether it could rise above it all. I had been in tough situations before—disasters, disarray, chaos, even war—but this was different. Here the stakes weren't just operational; they were deeply personal. Every decision touched the lives of animals and the people who cared for them.

I didn't arrive with a grand new vision. I began with what I've learned in every leadership role: you must earn trust before you can inspire change. That means listening—truly listening—to staff, volunteers, donors, and the community, then translating what I heard into a clear, focused, effective strategy combined with dogged determination. I formed a PACT with the staff and challenged them to build that same PACT with volunteers: *Performance, Accountability, Communication, Trust*. That foundation became our culture—and our compass.

What follows are seven principles that guided our transformation and that can help any organization build resilience.

1. Lead with Transparency

One of my first steps was to make the budget transparent. After studying it closely, I shared hard truths with the Board: their projection of a small deficit fell short—the actual gap was much greater and would require aggressive action. I laid off 17% of the staff but significantly increased training. Investment in staff development had never been part of the culture.

Some of it was hard to hear, but tension and uncertainty shifted when people realized I wasn't there to spin a story. I was there to tell the truth, and together, we would fix it. That decisive action set the tone: nothing hidden, no surprises, no excuses.

Transparency may sting in the moment, but it's the surest way to build long-term trust. If something isn't working, we face it. If we've made a mistake, we own it. If we need help, we ask for it. Leading with honesty, ethics, and integrity—even when it's uncomfortable—creates a culture that can withstand the toughest storms.

2. Set Bold Goals

Momentum builds confidence. We needed to earn the community's trust through our actions, not just our promises. Everyone wants to be part of a winning team. So, we set a bold goal and told the community exactly what we would accomplish: we would strive to build a no-kill community.

People responded—not just with money, but with energy, engagement, and a renewed sense of ownership in the mission.

3. Rise to Challenges Together

That renewed spirit came into sharp focus during our first summer together in 2012. May had been a difficult month. The summer "bully," euthanasia, had hit us hard. June looked even worse. Staff confidence was faltering.

I gathered the team and told them I believed in them. We would try new things, beginning with trusting and relying on our community. We launched an emergency appeal—not for funds, but for homes. We waived adoption fees for every animal, demonstrating to the community that we were willing to try anything to save them.

And they came—by the hundreds, from every walk of life. Families opened their homes to pets they hadn't planned for, staff and volunteers skipped meals and breaks to keep adoptions moving, and pride swelled as people saw history being made. For the first time, the shelter was emptied—an unimaginable milestone.

That moment changed everything. Staff who had been weary now felt a sense of pride. Volunteers who had previously doubted now felt a sense of ownership. Even families who already had pets stepped up, making room for "just one more." Then, our team reached out to shelters across the state, inviting them to send us their animals—I couldn't have been more proud.

It was the turning point for our organization, our staff, our volunteers, and our community. Having stood up to the "bully," we drew a line in the sand: never again would it be breached.

4. Empower the Team

I've always believed that when you give people a clear vision and trust them to be part of the solution, they rise to the challenge. In the Greater Charleston area, that meant empowering our team to make decisions at every level. From spay/neuter and adoption strategies to fundraising innovation and beyond, staff knew they had my support to try new approaches, even if some ideas failed.

The goal wasn't perfection; it was progress. Confidence—not arrogance—built a process that led to accomplishment.

5. Keep Focus Amid Criticism

Criticism is part of the territory in animal welfare. I don't ignore it, but I don't let it dictate the course, either. First, I ask whether it's rooted in truth or misunderstanding. If it's true, we fix it. If it's a misunderstanding, we communicate better. If it's rooted in hate, we stand up to it.

Either way, the mission—not the noise—guides our direction. You can't chase every opinion, or you'll grind to a halt, distracted from the critical work of lifesaving.

6. Stay Anchored to the Mission

Over the years, I've seen how easily our field can get tangled in politics, trends, partisanship, and egos. The work is demanding and emotional, but if we ground our decisions in ethics rather than ego, we won't just endure—we'll create lasting change.

Leadership isn't about titles, recognition, or being in "the club." It's about showing up every day, making decisions with integrity, and keeping the mission moving forward. It's about challenging and supporting the people driving the work and believing in them. The power of belief is unstoppable. Too often, I've seen frontline staff and supervisors undermined because no one believed in them. I vowed never to let that happen.

7. Build Beyond the Leader

One of my core beliefs is that a leader's job is to build something that lasts beyond their own tenure. I measure success by whether the organization can thrive without me. That's why I invest in people, systems, and a culture that doesn't hinge on one personality.

That philosophy was tested during multiple emergency deployments after hurricanes. As shelters in low-lying areas had to be evacuated, our team accepted responsibility: if an animal needed help and we could, we would. Our systems held. People knew their roles, trusted each other, and made decisions not in a vacuum, but in concert with one another.

That's when I knew the organization could stand on its own two feet, no matter who was at the helm. Or, as I often say, if you leave and everything collapses, you weren't really leading. You were just holding it together with your own two hands.

Leaving a Legacy That Matters

When the spotlight fades and the applause is gone, what remains is the culture you've built, the lives you've touched, and the mission you've strengthened. Legacy isn't measured in titles or tenures—it's measured in systems that hold, people who thrive, and communities that trust the work. That's the legacy worth leaving.

As I think back on this work, I'm most grateful for the people who made it possible—the staff who showed up with grit, the volunteers who gave without hesitation, and the community who believed in us even when the odds were long. I feel honored to be on this journey with them, and I know there is always more to learn, more to build, and more lives to touch, together.

***Joe Elmore** joined Charleston Animal Society in Charleston, South Carolina, as its CEO in 2012. He brought 25 years of experience in the nonprofit sector, spanning nine states and three international posts, to an organization in turmoil. He stabilized operations, led it to become a national model for lifesaving success and built the first no-kill community in the Deep South. He guided the shelter to becoming South Carolina's top-rated nonprofit for 14 consecutive years. And, in February 2023, he led Charleston Animal Society's VAX-A-PALOOZA campaign, which set a Guinness World Record for the most pledges received for a pet vaccination campaign in 24 hours, collecting 2,226 pledges and breaking the previous record of 1,867.*

Having served as CEO of five nonprofit organizations and COO of a national nonprofit, Elmore has devoted his life to defending and caring for the most vulnerable—abused children, at-risk youth, disaster victims, casualties of war, victims of HIV/AIDS, and abused or unwanted animals. Academically trained in engineering, he has applied problem-solving skills to social challenges, specializing in crisis management and organizational turnarounds, always leading with integrity, discipline, and a focus on results.

Elmore has been recognized by the Governors of Washington and the U.S. Virgin Islands, received the American Red Cross Tiffany Award for Management Excellence, and was awarded the U.S. Department of Defense Medal for his service in America's first Persian Gulf Conflict. In 2015, he was named one of nine national Maddie's Heroes in its inaugural class for inspirational and innovative leadership.

By investing in people, strengthening systems, and fostering trust, Elmore has built an enduring foundation at Charleston Animal Society—one that continues to serve as a model for animal welfare organizations nationwide.

Elmore shares his home with his companion, Boo, a puppy mill survivor rescued by Charleston Animal Society's lifesaving team.

"When we frame our needs in the context of city goals, we build credibility. We're no longer just 'the animal people.' We're public servants who understand the full system."

Josh Fisher

At the Table and in the Plan: Five Ways to Embed Animal Welfare into City Systems

When you lead animal services for the 14th largest city in the country, you quickly realize you're not just in animal welfare anymore—you're in government. That means navigating budgets, policies, elected officials, and many competing priorities. But it also means you have a chance to create real change—if you know how to speak the language and earn a seat at the table.

And that seat at the table isn't just about being in the room—it's about showing up where it matters: when city policies are drafted, when plans are shaped, when departments are asked to collaborate, when leadership priorities are set, and when budgets are decided. Each of these tables presents an opportunity to align your work with broader city goals—and to establish lasting systems that benefit both people and pets.

Speaking the Language of Government

I have spent over a decade leading *Charlotte-Mecklenburg Animal Care & Control* in Charlotte, North Carolina. I started like many others in our field—boots on the ground, deep in the work, passionate about helping animals. But leadership demanded a shift. I had to stop thinking only about field services or veterinary care and start thinking like a city leader.

That meant understanding what elected officials care about and tying our work to those priorities. For example, one of our city council members ran on a platform that emphasized strong housing initiatives. I tied our mission to hers: showing how people experiencing homelessness often decline housing because they can't bring their pets. That pet might be their only source of companionship—or their reason for waking up in the morning. We advocated for pet-friendly, affordable housing to remove that barrier.

What does that look like? We show up early. We ask: How many units in this new affordable housing project are pet-friendly? What would it take to increase that number? We talk to developers, zoning officials, city staff, and the city manager's office. We are there from the start to ensure that unhoused people have access to housing that includes their pets.

Connecting Animal Services to Citywide Goals

When you step into leadership, your perspective must shift. You can't do the new job with ideas from your old job. You have to take a 30,000-foot view to see how your teams work together as well as how your work connects with the rest of the city's agenda. Internally, I can't focus solely on the vet department, as if I were still a veterinary technician. I need to observe how the vet techs interact with the kennel staff and the adoption staff. I need to ensure everyone has the resources they need to perform their jobs more effectively.

With the City, we have to do the same. However, in this instance, we are examining different City Departments and identifying how our work affects theirs. Public health. Housing. Transportation. Social services. Animal services. These don't stand alone. We're a thread in the larger fabric of government. The more clearly we can articulate that connection, the more effective we become.

Our job is to make a compelling case for investment. This means utilizing data, modeling impact, and demonstrating how our work aligns with broader citywide objectives. And just as importantly, we need to demonstrate that we belong in the same rooms as other department leaders—whether we're talking about transportation corridors or public health equity.

That kind of strategic thinking was shaped by my involvement in the city's leadership team, where we explored how to run the business of government. I have taken lessons from that space and applied them directly to our work—because animal welfare is both a mission and a business. We may be compassion-driven, but we are not an enterprise fund. We don't generate revenue like aviation or utilities. We are a net cost. But we're still essential.

Becoming Part of the System

Since joining *Charlotte-Mecklenburg Animal Care & Control*, we have embedded animal services into public health efforts. When people apply for WIC (Special Supplemental Nutrition Program for Women, Infants, and Children) or food stamps, they're now asked if they have pets and whether they need food or other support. We don't want them using their WIC benefits to buy pet food if we have food available from the food pantry that we can give them instead. That information comes to us, and we follow up with vaccines, spaying and neutering, and access to food pantries.

For residents entering subsidized housing, we take an additional step by providing services in advance. We will spay or neuter their pet, vaccinate and microchip them, and hold onto the records for them. We then send copies of the pet's medical records directly to the housing agency. That means when a person is offered housing, that box is already checked—their pet is cleared to come with them. It's one less hurdle for someone already navigating a complex system.

This is what municipal shelters can do when they are fully integrated into the community. We remove barriers. We stay connected to other departments. We anticipate needs so that people and their pets can stay together.

Respecting That There Are Competing Priorities

When I need more animal care staff, I don't walk into a city budget meeting saying, *"We're short-staffed."* It's essential to clearly explain your department's needs while also acknowledging that other departments have competing priorities. That's hard, because our department is dealing with lives, and for us that can feel like the only priority. But, we have to recognize that the city budget involves more than just animal services and that the community has other pressing needs.

A few years ago, I learned that if you called 911, you might get a busy signal. As a citizen, I don't want to call 911 and get a busy signal. Clearly, we need more 911 telecommunicators. So, I walked into the budget meeting with city leaders and said, *"I know public safety is your top priority. If it's between us and 911 dispatchers, hire the dispatchers. But let me show you how our work also protects public safety and builds community trust to see if there is a way we can get both."*

When we frame our needs in the context of city goals, we build credibility. We're no longer just *"the animal people."* We're public servants who understand the whole system.

Letting Go to Lead

One of the most challenging lessons in leadership is realizing that when you transition into leading an organization, you're no longer the subject matter expert. That's your management staff's role. Your role is to surround yourself with experts and give them what they need to succeed. You are now responsible for everything—kennel operations, customer experience, community outreach, budgeting, staffing, and systems integration.

I had to learn to shift from being deep in the details to seeing how all the parts of our operation connected—and how they connected to the city's priorities. This isn't just about strategy; it's about trust. I trust my team to lead in their areas of expertise, and they trust me to remove obstacles and advocate for what they need.

You can't lead with tunnel vision. You have to zoom out. You have to step back so others can step up. You must understand how your department fits into the broader structure of local government.

Tips for Getting—and Keeping—Your Seat at the Table

Here's what I would share with any municipal leader trying to elevate animal services:

→ **Do your research.** Know what your council members ran on. Know their committee assignments. Frame your conversations around their priorities.

→ **Speak like a government leader.** Use data. Talk about policy. Make the case for your department's impact in citywide terms.

→ **Zoom out.** Don't build policy around one-off incidents. Look for patterns. Get to the root cause of the problems.

→ **Professionalize.** Show that animal services is a serious, well-run part of government, not just a passion project.

→ **Don't wait to be invited.** Reach out to other departments. Ask how you can support their goals. That's how partnerships—and respect—begin.

Having a seat at the table isn't about titles or turf. It's about doing the work in a way that aligns with the bigger picture. It's about translating compassion into strategy. It's about ensuring our voice is heard in the rooms where decisions are made, because our work supports the people, pets, and systems that shape our communities.

***Josh Fisher, Ph.D.,** is a nationally respected leader in animal welfare with over two decades experience, spanning private practice, corporate veterinary care, public health, and healthcare administration, with advanced training in informatics (the use of data and technology to improve health outcomes). He currently serves as Director of Animal Services for the City of Charlotte-Mecklenburg Animal Services in Charlotte, North Carolina, where he leads innovative efforts to protect public health, reunite pets and people, and build humane, sustainable communities.*

With a diverse educational background in population medicine, veterinary sciences, and public health, Dr. Fisher is known for bridging disciplines to solve complex animal welfare challenges. His leadership has helped transform systems through intake reduction strategies, advanced marketing and placement models, and strategic long-term planning. A passionate advocate for professional development, he invests heavily in the next generation of animal welfare leaders through mentorship, continued education, and cutting-edge research.

Dr. Fisher is the immediate past president of the National Animal Care & Control Association, serves on the Managing Executive Committee of the Human Animal Support Services Project, and is secretary/treasurer of the Academic & Practice-Based Research Section of the North Carolina Public Health Association. His achievements include a Ph.D. in veterinary science, certification as a Certified Animal Welfare Administrator, Certified Customer Experience Executive (CXE), and completion of the Best Friends Executive Leadership Program.

Throughout his career, Dr. Fisher has remained committed to improving outcomes for both animals and the communities they live in—always focused on helping both ends of the leash.

"Tomorrow is truly a new day—for them, for me, and for every one of us doing hard work in a hard world."

23

Inga Fricke

Find Your Family of Ducks

Working in animal welfare is hard.

We see the worst of humanity, carry too much work on too few shoulders, and try to help far too many innocent victims who need our care. And despite our deep commitment to the cause—and the sacrifices we and our loved ones make, so we can keep going—we're often met with criticism, harassment, and even vilification. Sometimes the hardest hits come from within our own community.

It's easy to feel overwhelmed, like nothing we do will ever be right or good enough. And in those moments, we start to wonder why we keep doing this work at all.

My best advice? *Find your little family of ducks.*

I still remember my first set of law school final exams. I was convinced I was going to fail miserably—and that, by extension, my entire life would fall apart. I pictured myself getting kicked out of school, slinking back to my parents' basement, and (if I was lucky) maybe getting a job as a grocery bagger at the local ShopRite. Oma, my German grandmother, always said I was good at that!

Okay, I was being a little dramatic.

In a panic, I went for a walk to clear my head. I couldn't shake the sense of doom. But then I came across a little pond, where a family of ducks was swimming along, blissfully unaware of my academic crisis. They were just doing their duck things, living their duck lives.

And that's when it hit me: If I came back tomorrow—after failing my first exam—those ducks would still be there. And after I failed my second exam? Still swimming. And even after I failed out completely, moved home in shame, and started wearing my ShopRite smock? Yup, still there.

The truth was, my success or failure in law school wouldn't impact 99.99% of the world, not even a little. That realization shouldn't have felt so profound—but somehow, it was. Watching that little duck family helped me put things back in perspective. They snapped me out of my funk and helped me re-center. I still thought I might fail. But I no longer believed the world would end if I did. (Spoiler alert: I passed my exams. And later? I left the legal field entirely to work in animal sheltering. I know—after all that drama!)

But here's the part that stuck: In every chapter of my life since, when things feel heavy or hopeless, I remember that little family of ducks. I remind myself that they'll still be there, paddling peacefully through the pond, no matter how my crisis plays out. They help me remember that I don't have to take myself so seriously. The hard moments will pass. Tomorrow really is a new day—for them, for me, and for every one of us doing hard work in a hard world.

As leaders, we set the tone not only for ourselves, but for our teams. If we can show them perspective, resilience, and hope—even through a simple story—we make the hard days survivable. When we remind our teams to zoom out, breathe, and see the bigger picture, we give them the same gift the ducks once gave me: perspective. And that's what allows us to endure the hardest days and still move this work forward, together.

Inga Fricke, J.D., *discovered her path to animal welfare leadership after several years as an environmental attorney, when volunteering in shelters and wildlife rehabilitation revealed where her true passion lay. She gained hands-on experience with the Wyandot County*

Humane Society and Loudoun County Animal Care and Control before joining the Humane Society of the United States (HSUS) in 2010 (currently known as the Humane World for Animals). There, she played a key role in supporting animal welfare professionals nationwide, helping launch Spayathon™ for Puerto Rico and contributing to widely used best-practice resources, including Adopters Welcome.

After leaving HSUS, Fricke became Director of Community Initiatives at Humane Pennsylvania, where she continued building programs that expanded access to care and strengthened community engagement. Today, she serves as Executive Director of the McKamey Animal Center in Chattanooga, Tennessee, leading with a focus on innovation, collaboration, and sustainability.

Fricke also lends her expertise at the national level, serving on the boards of the National Animal Control Association, the Animal Care and Control Association of Tennessee, and the Access to Veterinary Care Coalition. She is also an adjunct professor in Canisius University's Anthrozoology Department, where she helps prepare the next generation of leaders in the field.

"Anyone can run a shelter, but real leadership is about seeing the bigger picture—where we've been, where we are, and where we need to go. My job is to create a vision, empower people, and ensure that vision becomes reality."

Jon Gary

A Career Forged in Leadership and Lifesaving Change

I never intended to work in animal welfare. My background was in steel fabrication—welding, working with my hands, and building things that were strong and enduring. I assumed my career would follow that path. But in 1999, when the steel company I worked for shut down, I found myself looking for a job.

A colleague mentioned that the Oklahoma City animal shelter was hiring kennel cleaners. It wasn't what I envisioned for my future, but I had a family to support. I applied and got the job.

Initially, I viewed it as a temporary position. I planned to do the work, collect a paycheck, and move on. But the deeper I immersed myself in the shelter, the harder it became to walk away. I had spent my life building things, but at the shelter, I realized I could build something even more impactful—a better system, a stronger safety net for animals, and a more effective way to serve the community.

Six months into the job, I was promoted to shelter supervisor. I had been a supervisor in the steel industry, so I thought, *"Why not?"* That's when I truly saw the potential for change.

Gaining Perspective through Doing

When I stepped into leadership in 1999, Oklahoma City's shelter was a grim place. The live release rate was less than 10%, and animals were euthanized in gas chambers, an outdated and inhumane practice. I couldn't change policy overnight, but I paid attention, asked questions, and identified opportunities to shift the culture.

In 2001, we successfully eliminated gas chambers in favor of humane euthanasia methods—a critical first step. But I knew we needed more than policy changes. We needed an entirely new approach to sheltering.

I didn't come into leadership with a grand plan. I learned by doing. I transitioned from shelter supervisor to veterinary assistant, then to field services supervisor, and finally back to shelter operations. I wanted to understand every aspect of the system. The only way to lead effectively was to know the challenges firsthand.

That experience gave me a broad perspective on animal welfare, from the needs of the pets to the realities of field services. It shaped how I approached leadership, not as someone dictating from the top, but as someone who had walked every level of the job and knew what needed to change.

Building Programs That Last

Authentic leadership isn't about quick fixes. It's about creating solutions that endure long after you leave. Throughout my 25 year career in Oklahoma City, I developed programs that have permanently reshaped the city's approach to animal welfare.

One of the most impactful was our free spay/neuter program. Unlike many assistance programs, this one had no income restrictions. If you lived in Oklahoma City, you could have your pet sterilized for free. We partnered with a high-volume clinic to handle surgeries, with the city providing funding and oversight. The results were staggering:

→ More than 6,000 free spay/neuter surgeries were performed annually.

→ Intake at the shelter dropped by 8,000 to 9,000 animals per year.

→ A long-term reduction was seen in euthanasia rates.

The second major shift occurred in 2017, when I advocated for a community cat program. Before that, many stray cats brought into the shelter were euthanized. By implementing TNR strategies, we saw an immediate impact:

→ The live release rate for cats jumped from 68% to over 90%.

→ The shelter took in 3,000 fewer cats per year.

→ Lifesaving became the expectation, not the exception.

Programs like these succeed because they address the root causes of shelter overpopulation. They don't just reduce intake for a year or two; they create systemic, sustainable change. That is what leadership is about.

But leadership is also about making tough decisions. In 2017, Oklahoma City experienced a fatal dog mauling. We had to reassess our dangerous dog policies, tighten ordinances, and take a stronger approach to public safety. As a result, we cut the number of dangerous dog cases in half. It wasn't just about saving animals; it was about protecting the community while maintaining a balance of public trust and lifesaving efforts.

The Next Challenge: San Antonio

After 25 years in Oklahoma City, I had reached the highest position I could within the organization and planned to retire. I had built programs, changed policies, and shaped a culture that prioritized lifesaving. But I knew I had more to give.

When I was recruited for the Director position at San Antonio Animal Care Services, I wasn't actively looking to leave Oklahoma. My entire family was there—siblings, nieces, nephews, even a grandchild. But I also knew that if I was going to leave, it had to be for the right opportunity.

San Antonio faces unique challenges. The shelter takes in 8,000–9,000 more dogs per year than Oklahoma City, yet it has half the kennel space. The demand is relentless, and the staff is working at capacity. And while the city has made progress, the biggest challenge remains—balancing public safety with live outcomes.

I knew this wouldn't be easy, but I also knew I was ready.

Cultivating Strategic Leadership

Leading in this environment requires a delicate balance between pragmatism and innovation. There are three critical areas I'm focused on:

→ **Managing Dangerous Dogs**: Public safety is paramount. We must aggressively address roaming and aggressive dogs while also supporting responsible pet owners.

→ **Improving Live Outcomes for Dogs**: The shelter has made tremendous progress in cat lifesaving, but dog intake remains high. We need to expand foster care, increase rescue partnerships, and reevaluate shelter operations to improve outcomes.

→ **Expanding Capacity**: The shelter was not built to handle the volume of animals it receives. We must advocate for increased resources, better infrastructure, and community-driven solutions to reduce intake at the source.

These challenges are not insurmountable. The staff at San Antonio ACS is deeply committed, and the city is invested in making improvements. My role is to bring all the pieces together—staff, leadership, policy, and community support—to build a system that works.

A Leadership Philosophy Rooted in Action

Throughout my career, I've learned that the best leaders are not just visionaries. They are doers. Change doesn't happen because of a title or a position. It happens when you understand every aspect of an organization, engage the right people, and execute a plan that works in the real world.

My leadership philosophy is simple:

→ Understand every level of the operation—from cleaning kennels to crafting policy.

→ Listen to the people doing the work—they often have the best solutions.

→ Never be afraid to challenge the status quo—progress requires discomfort.

→ Data matters—track results and adjust based on what works.

→ Build programs that last—change should be structural, not situational.

Most importantly, I believe that real leaders create other leaders. The success of any shelter, any program, or any movement depends on empowering the next generation to step up, innovate, and push the boundaries of what's possible.

Shaping the Leaders of Tomorrow

In animal welfare, the real measure of leadership isn't just the programs we build, it's the people we inspire to continue the work long after we're gone. The future of this field depends on passionate individuals who are willing to step up, challenge the status quo, and implement real, lasting change.

The truth is, leadership isn't about waiting for the perfect job title. It's about recognizing a problem and taking action. It's about taking responsibility, finding solutions, and making decisions that push the field forward. It's about learning every aspect of this work—whether you're cleaning kennels, managing intake, working in field services, or leading an entire organization.

If you're in this field today, you're already in a position to lead. The question is: *how will you use that position*?

→ Will you advocate for more effective policies that improve outcomes for both animals and people?

→ Will you support your team and help them grow into strong, capable professionals?

→ Will you challenge outdated practices and advocate for more effective and humane solutions?

→ Will you stay focused on the big picture, knowing that every small action contributes to a larger movement?

The best leaders don't wait to be asked. They earn it through action. They step up, take risks, and make things happen. And most importantly, they empower others to do the same.

The next generation of animal welfare leaders is already here. They are the kennel attendants who pay attention, the vet techs who go the extra mile, the field officers who problem-solve in real time, and the shelter managers who embrace innovation.

Wherever you are in your career, your leadership journey starts now. Be bold. Be relentless. And never lose sight of why you're here—to make a difference, one life at a time.

***Jon Gary** is a seasoned animal welfare leader with more than 25 years of experience transforming municipal sheltering. In late 2024, he relocated with his wife, two of their four children, and three dogs to become Director of Animal Care Services (ACS) in San Antonio, Texas, a move he embraced as both a personal and professional challenge following decades of success in Oklahoma City.*

Gary's career began in 1999 with what was meant to be a temporary kennel-cleaning job at the Oklahoma City Animal Shelter. Within six months, he was promoted to shelter supervisor, eventually rising to Superintendent (the equivalent of Director). Under his leadership, Oklahoma City saw major improvements in animal welfare, including a citywide free spay/neuter program that reduced shelter intake by nearly 9,000 animals annually and a community cat program that increased the feline live-release rate from 68% to over 90%.

In San Antonio, Gary oversees the city's animal welfare operations, including enforcing ordinances, protecting public health and safety, expanding placement and retention programs, and fostering partnerships to strengthen the human-animal bond. He is certified as an animal cruelty investigator through the University of Missouri's

National Animal Cruelty Investigations School, holds shelter operations certification from the American Humane Association, has a Pets for Life training accreditation from Humane World for Animals (formerly the Humane Society of the United States), and is a graduate of the Best Friends Executive Leadership Certification Program.

A lifelong advocate for staff well-being and animal welfare, Gary values building strong teams that create lasting change. Outside of work, he enjoys unwinding over a game of pool and spending time with his family and three dogs.

"The best leaders aren't the ones who never stumble; they're the ones who take responsibility and adjust course."

Nicholas Gilman

Management Malfunctions: A Guide to Recognizing and Owning Your Mistakes

Next year will be my 41st year in animal welfare. Almost all that time has been spent in managerial or leadership roles. And, I have made every mistake in the book over those years. Consistency is key.

Everyone makes mistakes, of course. The fact is that making a mistake here and there is okay. But if you are incapable of recognizing your occasional error, then that is a far greater concern. The issue in leadership is not whether you will make mistakes (you will), it's about what you do about them and how you avoid repeating the same one.

"Well, I don't make a lot of mistakes."

Nah, you probably do. However, it is possible that you don't admit to having made them, even to yourself. That, in itself, is a mistake and a fairly costly one at that. After all, executives in leadership positions often work in an echo chamber. None of their subordinates will tell them what mistakes they are making. Therefore, we must acknowledge our own mistakes as we proceed. The person who cannot admit fault is likely to keep repeating errors.

One trick I employ when it becomes evident that something has gone wrong is to assess my degree of responsibility for the issue. If I own only five percent of the issue, then my next step is to focus *solely on that 5 percent*. When I do, I often find that if I had not committed whatever that five percent was, the rest of the problem—the 95 percent—may never have ensued. It is extremely important that a leader can own the issue and not just assign the problem to others.

Another trick in determining one's own accountability is to ask yourself: if you could go back in time, what would you have done differently? If your answer suggests that, given a second chance, you would have said or done something differently, then you are getting closer to admitting there was some fault in your actions.

"Ok, I made a mistake. Now what?"

That's okay. Own it! Make sure to acknowledge your error, certainly to yourself if not others. If apologies are in order, make those. Be sincere even if you don't own the whole ball of wax. People are forgiving of errors if one is contrite. Own it, apologize, and move on. A good leader isn't going to quibble over whether other people contributed to the issue; a good leader will accept responsibility for all of it.

"Are there unforgivable mistakes?"

The ones that may be harder to forgive are those related to behavior. Dishonesty, contributing to a hostile work environment, sexual misconduct, losing one's temper, etc. Those are types of behaviors that disqualify someone from being considered a strong, suitable leader. Mistakes, such as forgetting to attend a meeting or copying someone on an email they shouldn't have received, are also mistakes, but we learn from them. Bad behavior, on the other hand, is very difficult for a leader to overcome and rightly so.

"I take pride in showing how I react to news. Am I doing something wrong?"

Leaders need to be trusted not to overreact to news, good or bad. When the boss reacts demonstrably to bad news by becoming upset, getting angry, or looking for someone to blame, their staff will eventually learn not to bring them bad news in the first place. Of course, bad news still happens, but no one wants to include the reactionary boss in the matter until it is too late. The corollary is that leaders who accept all manner of news with calm equanimity are those whom the staff trust to hear the good and the bad. In other words, we should be *responding* (and, calmly at that) to news, not *reacting* strongly to it.

"As the leader, I am the face of the organization! Is that wrong?"

This is a difficult concept. Should the leader always be the public face of the organization? While that may be the default, a good leader will look for opportunities for others in the organization to be on stage. Major announcements should come from the leader, of course. But what about leading all-staff meetings? Radio, social media, or podcasts about the animal of the month? Does the leader *always* have to be the only one the public sees? And, if so, is that because that is what the organization needs, or is that what the fragile ego of the leader needs? After all, the public needs to see the whole organization as leaders, not just the person with the title.

"Should I be leading an evolution or a revolution?"

There are times when a leader does not see the need for a revolution, but rather continuing evolution. I regret once having accepted an interim position with an organization that was failing financially and operationally. While I did my best to help them evolve into an organization that would succeed, what I really needed to do was to tell them that their course was unsustainable. They truly needed to, not just make adjustments, but to completely reassess everything from their board of directors to what their functions really needed to be, considering their complete lack of resources. They needed to *revolutionize* their organization. I should either not have accepted the position or, once in place, should have made it clear that the very composition of the organization needed to radically change. My mistake was in not recommending revolution, regardless of whether the board wanted to hear it or not.

"I am the leader. Should the staff adapt to me?"

In movies and popular culture, the leader is often portrayed as a square-jawed, independent, and forthright individual who leads with grim determination and expects those who work for them to follow without complaint. What nonsense. That is a Hollywood conceit and one that rarely works outside of a movie.

One of a leader's primary responsibilities is to ensure that all of his/her staff succeed on their own, and not just because they are following you. This means understanding each staff member's approach to their job. Let your jaw be as square as you want, but be careful about the "independent" part. To lead successfully in today's environment, a good leader needs to understand what motivates each member of their staff. Some staff will need daily meetings and encouragement. Others will respond best to as few one-on-one meetings as possible. How to motivate a team of managers (unless you are in a World War II movie) means understanding how your managers tick. That requires a willingness to tailor your approach to leadership to the needs of your staff. And, the mistake that can be made here is thinking that your superior leadership will overcome all. Superior leadership is fine, but truly understanding and relating to your direct reports is what makes leadership effective. That requires emotional intelligence.

"So, making mistakes is not a failure on my part?"

Leaders make mistakes. We all make mistakes. That is not failure unless we cannot acknowledge our mistakes. Sometimes there is that question in an interview where you are asked, *"What is your greatest fault,"* and you answer something like, *"I am too much of an overachiever,"* or some other self-gratifying compliment that avoids the question. This suggests that you may not fully understand where, as a leader, you are making mistakes. In my case, for example, I have a memory that fails me, so I compensate for that by working with staff who have great memories. I am not a detail-oriented person, so I compensate for that by selecting teammates who are great detail-oriented individuals.

Admit your mistakes, and let your shortcomings (we all have them) help determine how you work with your staff. If we are truthful and decent leaders, our staff will quietly acknowledge our mistakes and be all the more instrumental in helping us lead.

__Nicholas Gilman__ has dedicated more than four decades to advancing animal welfare at the local, national, and international levels. His career began in animal shelters, where he worked in nearly every role, from direct animal care to executive director, giving him a deep understanding of both frontline challenges and organizational leadership. Over the years, he expanded his work to include national disaster relief, cruelty investigations, consulting, and shelter design.

Gilman worked for the Humane Society of the United States (currently known as Humane World for Animals) and the American Humane Association, where he served as Director of Animal Programs. A recognized voice in the field, he has been featured on the NBC Today Show, CBS This Morning, and National Public Radio, and has authored numerous articles in humane trade publications. He has also presented hundreds of workshops on sheltering and animal protection issues across the United States and abroad, and was a founding board member of the National Federation of Humane Societies.

In 2006, Gilman founded Humane Logic, a consulting firm dedicated to strengthening nonprofit animal organizations through strategic planning, interim leadership, board development, and organizational review. His contributions have been honored with the Dennis J. White Award for Excellence in Instruction and Training from the American Humane Association and the Humanitarian of the Year Award from the Wisconsin Federation of Humane Societies.

Today, Gilman serves as Executive Director of Second Chance Humane Society in Ridgway and Telluride, Colorado, where he continues to apply his lifetime of experience to improve the lives of animals.

"Shelters are incredibly emotional places—full of urgency, heartbreak, and hope. If the energy isn't carefully managed, it can tip into burnout and conflict."

Jason Gluck

From Spotlights to Second Chances: What It Taught Me About Leading People and Saving Pets

When people learn that I spent the first part of my career managing some of the most high-profile entertainers in the world before becoming the CEO at Furry Friends Humane in Jupiter, Florida, they're typically shocked. The two fields—the glitz and glamor of show business and the grind of animal sheltering—seem worlds apart. Yet to me, the throughline couldn't be clearer. Whether guiding a Grammy winner or leading a lifesaving organization, success depends almost entirely on strategy and the human connection.

Like entertainment, animal welfare has its own demand for relentless creativity and innovation. The lessons I learned navigating the world of record-breaking tours, licensing and merchandising contracts, and artistic egos have shaped every decision I've made as a nonprofit leader. The parallels between the two worlds are striking. Whether managing a world tour or a nonprofit team, the principles of leadership, balance, and purpose remain the same.

Lesson 1
Managing Energy is as important as Managing People

In the entertainment industry, the stakes are continually high. One misstep can spread around the world in minutes. I quickly saw that managing talent wasn't purely about logistics; it was about managing the energy of the artist, the support team, the fans, and, of course, myself. A career can be made or broken by the mood at a single point in time.

That same applies to animal welfare work. You know all too well that shelters are incredibly emotional places. They are full of urgency, heartbreak, and hope. Staff and volunteers hold the weight of what they see each day. If the energy isn't carefully managed, it can tip into burnout and conflict.

As a leader, I set the tone. Just as I once worked to keep a team inspired on their umpteenth show in a given month, I now ensure our shelter staff feel supported and valued despite constant requests for intakes, assistance, and their time. Leaders must model resilience, provide space for decompression, and bring moments of joy and silliness (and my team will tell you I'm big on the latter!). Energy spreads quickly; if you want a team that stays motivated, you must model the optimism you expect them to carry forward.

Lesson 2
Precision and Planning are Non-Negotiable

In entertainment, details matter. This level of precision isn't about control, though; it's about respect for the audience who choose to spend their time and treasure with us.

I carry that same mindset into shelter operations. The public entrusts us with their animals, their donations, and their hopes for a more humane world. Sloppiness cannot be an option. Whether we are coordinating a multi-state transport through our Hope on Wheels program, building a humane education curriculum, providing a seamless and curated adoption experience, or hosting a fundraising gala, who we are is in the details. Staff t-shirts, smiles, and polished greetings for visitors—these are just a few of the elements that seem small, but for my team, they're nonnegotiable.

Experience has taught me that when people see excellence in the small things, they believe in your capacity to deliver on the big things. Spending your time on the details, such as how a meet and greet room feels when a potential adopter walks in, how a thank you letter to a donor is worded, and how a volunteer is appreciated, creates trust and confidence that extend well beyond a single moment.

Lesson 3
Crisis is a Test of Character

Entertainment, like animal welfare, is often plagued by crises. In my old life, there were broken-down tour buses, public controversies, and the feeling that, in any moment, things could be all over. My job often required that I step in during the most challenging times. I was there to stay calm and find solutions that protected the artist and the team.

In that way, leading a shelter is no different. There may be hurricanes, respiratory virus outbreaks, social media pile-ons, a transport vehicle breaking down on the highway, or an injured hog wandering onto your shelter grounds. Okay, that last one was highly specific, but for the most part, these are inevitable facts of life. (And, yes, we had once performed a miracle for a porky pig and placed him into a loving home.)

In these difficult times, your team doesn't just look to you for direction; they look at the core of who you are. And that requires some deep personal reflection. In those first instances of crisis, do you panic? Do you rush to blame? Do you lock yourself in a closet and scream? I'm here to tell you it's natural to do all of the above. But do it on your own time. As a leader, you have a singular task: to steady the ship and point the way forward.

At Furry Friends Humane, I've learned that our most challenging days are the ones that define us. A leader must remain composed, not because the situation isn't serious, but because clarity and calm create confidence and a virtuous circle where steadiness builds trust, trust strengthens the team, and a stronger team makes it possible to meet your challenge head-on. More than what you did to address the crisis, your team will remember how you carried yourself.

Lesson 4
Relationships Build Longevity

In entertainment, a good manager is the bridge connecting the artist with the record label, the promoters, the fans, and the media. Trust is the currency. I often found myself negotiating in high-pressure situations where the deal came down not to money, but to whether people believed I would keep my word.

That's equally true in animal welfare. Donors don't give purely because they love animals—in that case, they've got lots of options. They give because they believe in the people who are asking. Partner shelters don't accept transports because it's convenient—they accept them because we've built a reputation for sending healthy, behaviorally sound dogs and cats. Volunteers don't show up consistently for our organization because they have nowhere else to go—they come to us because we value and appreciate them.

At the heart of every successful nonprofit organization are relationships moored in trust, consistency, earnestness, and gratitude. Even more so than in entertainment, commitments in our field matter. Never overpromise and underdeliver. Keeping your word and being kind at all times, whether to a major foundation or a former staff member, allows you to build momentum that sustains the mission. No interaction is wasted, because anyone who finds their way into your orbit could become tomorrow's ally in saving lives.

Lesson 5
Storytelling Moves People

Managing entertainers taught me that facts don't fill arenas or sell albums, stories do. Fans connect not just to a song but to the narrative behind it. The heartbreak, the triumph, the journey is everything.

In animal welfare, numbers are essential. Live release rates, intake data, and everything in between truly do matter. But stories are what win hearts and minds. A dog seized during a cruelty case and then transported hundreds of miles for his second chance puts a face to the complex mass of data confronting us. That tiny anemic kitten who arrived at your shelter moments from death, and the medical team who dropped everything to give him a blood transfusion, resonate deeply not only with your supporters but also with the employees and volunteers who are the heartbeat of your work. As a leader, I must be both a strategist and a storyteller at all times, with emails to staff, social media posts, letters to donors. Every communication is an opportunity to tell your story.

Lesson 6
Start With "*Yes*"

Animal sheltering can be a risk-averse field, and understandably so. Mistakes can have grave consequences. But I've learned that saying no by default limits creativity and lifesaving potential. My philosophy is simple: I start with "*yes*," and ask my team to convince me why it should be a "*no*." This doesn't mean every idea moves forward. Sometimes, the correct answer is no. But beginning with "*yes*," forces us to explore solutions before shutting the door.

Some of our most impactful programs, including initiatives that once seemed too ambitious or complicated, came to life because I refused to take "*impossible*" or "*not viable*" at face value. In a field where lives hang in the balance every minute of every day, the courage to start with "*yes*" can make the most profound difference.

Final Thoughts

At Furry Friends Humane, I carry the lessons of my past life with me. That crazy world, often known for its shallowness, provided some very profound lessons in the value of precision, energy, centeredness, relationships, storytelling, and openness to change that will stay with me always. Yet nothing matches the work you and I share, which, at its core, is the simple and profound act of giving animals the second chances they deserve.

To new animal welfare leaders, I hope that, above all, you will honor the souls who depend on you. If you hold fast to that, everything else will find its place.

And to those who have walked this road far longer than I have, I know that every day still brings new lessons. To you, I offer a special word of thanks for undertaking this demanding yet endlessly rewarding work. The need never lets up, and weariness can come quickly, but your devotion sustains this field and all of us within it.

Jason Gluck's *journey from powerhouse media executive to trailblazing animal welfare leader spans two vastly different industries—both profoundly shaped by his visionary influence.*

In his early career, Gluck managed some of the world's most high-profile entertainers, playing a pivotal role in the development and global launch of Hannah Montana and Miley Cyrus. His work not only propelled Miley into international stardom but also transformed the franchise into one of Disney's most successful and award-winning properties. He also discovered pop sensation Sabrina Carpenter during a global talent search, which helped launch her career and cement his reputation for identifying and cultivating breakout stars. Gluck's work in entertainment earned recognition from The Webby Awards, Popstar!, and The Davey Awards, underscoring his talent for precision, planning, and innovation in fast-paced, high-stakes environments.

Today, Gluck channels that same visionary energy into animal welfare as Chief Lifesaving Officer & CEO of Furry Friends Humane in Jupiter, Florida. Drawing on the lessons of strategy, relationship-building, crisis management, and storytelling honed in the entertainment industry, he has transformed Furry Friends Humane into a nationally prominent organization. Under his leadership, Furry Friends Humane has expanded lifesaving programs, strengthened partnerships with other shelters, and established a reputation for excellence and compassion in animal care.

Gluck has also been nationally recognized for his impact on the sheltering field. He was honored with the Shelter Hero Leadership

Award from the Bissell Pet Foundation and PetSmart Charities, which celebrates the strength, determination, and compassion of leaders who consistently go above and beyond for animals in need. Known for his relentless creativity, energy, and optimism, Gluck continues to shape the future of animal welfare, leading with the same precision and vision that once built entertainment empires—now dedicated to giving animals the second chances they deserve.

"Leadership in the nonprofit world is not just about guiding an organization; it's about guiding people. It's about showing them that every small victory - every pet we sterilize, every family we keep together—adds up to something much bigger."

Bonnie Hill

From Crisis to Compassion: How Leadership and Vision Built a Lifesaving Legacy in Texas

When I first moved to the countryside outside of Dallas, I didn't know what awaited me. My husband and I had decided in 2003 to escape the hustle of city life to seek a quieter, simpler existence. We had purchased a beautiful property, and I was eager to enjoy the tranquility of rural living. However, as soon as we arrived at our new home, we were met with an unexpected and unsettling situation: ten puppies were waiting for us in the yard, left behind by the previous owner.

Naturally, I was upset they had been abandoned. These were living, breathing creatures, and there was no way I could just leave them. I immediately called the former owner to let him know that his puppies were still on the property. His response left me speechless—he told me I could bring them over, but he planned to drown them. The thought of these innocent puppies being killed in such a cruel way was something I couldn't fathom. At that moment, I realized just how dire the situation was for animals in this rural community. There were no shelters, no veterinary clinics, and no place to turn when animals were no longer wanted. It seemed the solution for this, and likely many other rural communities without resources, was simply to abandon them or kill them.

This experience inspired me to act. I began researching the issue of pet overpopulation and the lack of resources for animals in rural areas. I debated between starting an animal shelter or a spay-neuter clinic in Kaufman County. I quickly learned that spaying and neutering pets was one of the most effective ways to reduce the number of unwanted animals. Yet, at the time, there were no spay-neuter clinics nearby, and only one in Dallas—nearly 50 miles away—which was completely overwhelmed.

The more I researched, the more determined I became to address the problem. I realized that if I wanted to make a difference, I would need to start a nonprofit organization dedicated to providing spay and neuter services to the community. And so, in 2004, I founded the Kaufman County Animal Awareness Project, which today is known as Spay Neuter Network (SNN).

Building a Vision from the Ground Up

Building a nonprofit from scratch was both daunting and exhilarating. At first, it was just me and a handful of volunteers. We launched with a mobile spay-neuter unit that traveled around Kaufman County, providing surgeries and vaccinations to pet owners who couldn't afford traditional veterinary care. Over the 15 years, I served as executive director, we expanded our services and reach. We opened stationary clinics in Dallas, Fort Worth, and Crandall, and our mobile clinic continued to serve rural areas in North Texas where access to veterinary care was limited.

As the organization grew, so did our impact. We developed a transportation program that enabled us to pick up pets from low-income neighborhoods and rural communities, and transport them to our clinics for their surgeries. This program proved to be a game-changer, as it removed one of the biggest barriers financially challenged pet owners faced: transportation. Many of the people we serve didn't have cars, and even if they did, they couldn't afford to drive long distances to access veterinary care on the other side of town. By bringing spay-neuter services to them with the mobile clinic and bringing them to our clinics via the transport program, we prevented thousands of unwanted litters from being born and kept them out of shelters.

Leadership Lessons Learned Along the Way

Starting SNN not only changed the trajectory of my life but also transformed the lives of the people who came to work alongside me. My background was in medical sales and business, not animal welfare or nonprofit management. But I had a passion for solving problems, and the problem in front of me—preventing the suffering of unwanted pets—was something I couldn't ignore.

In the early days, I was deeply involved in every aspect of the operation—managing finances, booking clinic locations, and overseeing logistics. But as the organization grew, I realized I couldn't do it all. I had to trust my team to take on leadership roles themselves. Empowering others to step up wasn't just practical—it was vital for our success.

During that time, my leadership style wasn't always what it needed to be. If I'm being honest, I was often too direct and task-focused, prioritizing efficiency over connection. I didn't engage with staff as I should have and, at times, failed to recognize the emotional weight of the work we were doing. Coming from outside the animal welfare field, I had to learn for myself that this work is deeply emotional, and I needed to fully acknowledge how it was affecting me and the people around me.

Over time, I came to understand that people join this field because they care deeply about animals, and if they don't feel empowered to make a difference, they won't last long. I began to see that my task-focused approach wasn't enough to inspire or sustain the dedication needed for such challenging work. Recognizing this, I started making changes to my leadership style—embracing the team more fully, checking in on them regularly, and fostering a culture of support. This realization became one of my most significant leadership lessons: creating a culture where staff feel valued and motivated is essential to building a strong, resilient team. When people feel empowered, they go above and beyond for the animals we serve. They bring their best selves to the work, knowing their efforts truly matter. As my leadership skills developed, I made it a priority to instill a sense of purpose and ownership throughout our organization. I wanted every member of our team to know they were not just doing a job—they were an essential part of our life-saving mission.

From Crisis to Legacy

Building the organization taught me that every phase of its growth required a different approach—and that I had to develop new leadership skills at each stage. Leadership in the nonprofit world is not just about guiding an organization; it's about guiding people. It's about inspiring them to give their best, even when the work is hard and the challenges feel insurmountable. It's about showing them that every small victory—every pet we sterilize, every family we keep together—adds up to something much bigger. And it's about leading with compassion, not just for the animals we serve, but for the people who dedicate their lives to helping them.

I wasn't always that leader. I had a lot to learn and made plenty of mistakes managing people along the way. But every opportunity, every challenge, and every mistake helped me better understand what leadership could truly mean for the work we were doing and the people driving it forward.

In the end, building SNN has shaped me as a leader in ways I never could have anticipated. It has taught me the power of persistence, the value of collaboration, and the importance of compassion. It has shown me that authentic leadership is about lifting others up and empowering them to make a difference in the world. Together, we've built something far greater than I ever imagined when I first found those ten puppies in my yard—we've built a legacy of care, compassion, and community.

***Bonnie Hill** is an accomplished leader with a proven track record of creating impactful programs to address critical animal welfare issues. Her decades-long background in medical sales equipped her with the strategic and operational skills that proved invaluable when she recognized the urgent need to address pet overpopulation in her community and committed herself to solving it.*

In 2004, Hill founded an organization now known as Spay Neuter Network, a nonprofit focused on reducing pet overpopulation by providing affordable veterinary services in Kaufman County, Texas, and served as it's executive director for more than 14 years. What began as a small bi-weekly mobile clinic quickly grew under her leadership into a nationally recognized organization that today serves the Dallas-Fort Worth metroplex and San Antonio, Texas. SNN delivers critical care to underserved pet owners through spay-neuter clinics, mobile clinics, and a transport program that increases access to veterinary services in high-need communities.

Hill's results-driven approach and ability to manage complex projects were key to building SNN from the ground up. She successfully secured multimillion-dollar funding, maintained high standards of care, and fostered strong relationships with donors, public officials, and community partners. Her unique ability to translate private-sector skills into nonprofit impact enabled her to create innovative solutions that expanded access to care and improved the lives of both animals and their families.

Today, Hill continues her legacy as Grants Manager at the Empowerment Foundation, where she supports initiatives aligned with her lifelong commitment to creating healthier, more compassionate communities.

"We tell ourselves—and each other—that we have to act like we're fine... but if we can't be honest with each other, how can we get through the hard stuff?"

Sarah Hock

This Work Is Hard. Let's Say That Out Loud.

I've been in animal welfare for over 20 years, and I can honestly say I didn't know what kind of leader I wanted to be until the last six or seven years. That clarity didn't come from a workshop or a book—it came from struggle. It came from seeing the emotional toll our work takes on staff and recognizing that I had a responsibility to make things better.

Like some of us, I started as a volunteer. After graduating college with what I lovingly refer to as a "super useful" liberal arts degree, I took a job as a humane education instructor, running Girl Scout workshops and summer camps at the Arizona Animal Welfare League in Phoenix, Arizona. That was 2004.

Since then, I've worked my way through just about every corner of the field. I've been an executive director at a rural nonprofit, run low-cost veterinary clinics, managed grants at PetSmart Charities, and now, for the past six years, I've been the executive director at a municipal shelter, Joint Animal Services in Olympia, Washington. This is the first job that forced me to change how I think about leadership.

Culture Change Starts with Emotional Safety

When I moved from Arizona to Washington, I left behind my support network. I had to learn a new community, a new shelter culture, and a new landscape for animal welfare. It might sound silly, but even the customs were different. In Arizona, we were often sending animals—by the hundreds—to almost empty shelters in Washington. There, saving lives wasn't something they had to fight for every day. The urgency wasn't the same as it was for us in Arizona.

But the COVID-19 pandemic changed that. Suddenly, shelters across Washington had to catch up to what others had been doing for years. Progressive practices, such as TNR, were just beginning to take hold. I came into an organization that still had drop boxes (cages built into the wall where people could anonymously leave pets after hours). Some members of the community were furious when I shut them down. Even years later, I still get emails about it. The frustration wasn't just about the boxes, though. It was about change. Washington shelters and their communities had never been forced to change their practices before.

At the same time, I was trying to figure out how to lead a team that had already been through two extremes. One leader sided with the public over the staff to avoid conflict. The other made the public the enemy to protect the team. Both created toxic environments. No one had addressed the core issue: emotional safety. The freedom to have a bad day. To cry after a hard euthanasia. To disagree with your supervisor or admit when you don't understand a change.

It took years to rebuild the culture. Only in the last two have I really started to enjoy the work we've done as a team. Because now, people feel safe. They know they can take time off without guilt. They know they're allowed to ask questions and bring forward their ideas. They know I've got their backs.

When you build that kind of trust, it changes everything. Now, when a member of the public complains about a staff member, I usually know right away whether there's truth to it—because I know my team. I know their intentions. And even if someone had a bad day, we treat it as a coaching moment, not a disciplinary one. Unless it's unethical or violates city policy, we talk it through and figure out how to do better next time.

We also raised our animal care tech salaries by 24% last year—because they were still starting at minimum wage. Meanwhile, fast food workers were making more. These are people with emotionally taxing jobs. At the very least, they should be compensated fairly.

Vulnerability is the Real Leadership Tool

But for all the culture change and policy work, here's what I think matters most: vulnerability. Leadership isn't about having all the answers or holding it all together. And yet, we tell ourselves—and each other—that we have to act like we do.

When I first arrived, several of us initiated a monthly gathering for executive directors and CEOs in the region. A safe space for us to talk. And yet, even in that space, I've watched people I admired pretend everything was fine, only to send me an email later saying they had been let go. I had no idea they were struggling. They didn't feel safe enough to say so, not even to peers who understood the pressures they faced every day.

That's heartbreaking. Because if we can't be honest with each other, how can we get through the hard stuff?

So, here's my advice to new and aspiring leaders: find your circle of trust. People you can be real with. People who won't judge you when you're struggling. People who will tell you the truth, even when it's hard—especially when it's hard. We all need someone who'll give us a loving kick in the pants and a soft place to land. And we need to be those people for each other, too. That person for me is a work colleague whom I met about 11 years into my career. We have watched each other grow and supported one another through the hard stuff. She is who I turn to when I need a reality check.

We Can't Carry This Work Alone

This work is hard. Let's say that out loud. The emotions run deep. The public doesn't always understand, and sometimes they come after us in ways that are cruel and deeply personal. I've been harassed, doxed, and threatened. I've been called names I won't repeat. And like many of my colleagues, I've been told to just accept it—that it's part of the job.

But it shouldn't be. Compassion should not come at the cost of our well-being. We shouldn't have to choose between protecting our teams and protecting ourselves. We shouldn't have to pretend we're fine just to keep moving.

We can't change everything. But we can start by being honest—with ourselves, and with each other. We can stop pretending we're fine when we're not. We can be leaders who build trust, give feedback with kindness, and create spaces where people feel seen, supported, and safe.

That's the kind of leadership I've worked hard to practice. It's the kind I'm still learning. And it's the kind I hope others in our field feel empowered to embrace—so no one has to carry this work alone.

Because if we can show up for each other the way we show up for animals, the work we do won't just save lives, it will lift up the people doing the saving.

***Sarah Hock** is the Executive Director of Joint Animal Services in Olympia, Washington, where she oversees animal sheltering, field services, and community outreach for multiple jurisdictions. With over 20 years' experience in the animal welfare field, she brings extensive expertise in executive leadership, program development, strategic planning, capital campaigns, municipal and field services, and organizational development.*

A trailblazer in the field, Hock was among the first in the nation to earn an Executive Leadership Certificate through a collaboration between Best Friends Animal Society and Southern Utah University. Her leadership extends well beyond her own organization. She currently serves as President of the Washington Federation for Animal Care and Control Agencies and was recently elected to the Board of Directors for the National Animal Care and Control Association.

Hock is a strong advocate for professional development and industry growth, working to raise standards, promote best practices in field response, create positive outcomes for animals, and implement proactive community programming that keeps pets and people together. She prioritizes the safety and well-being of animal welfare professionals while fostering a culture of continuous improvement, innovation, and professionalization across the field.

Hock holds a Bachelor's degree in Fine Arts and a Master's Degree in Nonprofit Studies (MNS) from Arizona State University. Outside of work, Sarah enjoys gardening, traveling, and spending time with her family, which includes five cats and a lively flock of chickens.

"Good leaders are leaving the field because of emotional and personal attacks. This is leading to a loss of leadership in animal welfare. We need to rebuild and support leaders who understand the balance between compassion and strategy, and who have the resilience to keep moving forward."

Ed Jamison

Going from "Getting Through the Day" to "Winning the Day"

Momentum. That's the word I keep coming back to when I think about leadership in animal welfare. It's not just about moving forward—it's about setting goals, creating sustainable progress, and keeping everyone aligned toward a shared vision, even when the road gets rough.

In the early 2000s, my entry into animal welfare was almost accidental. I was working for a service department when an opportunity came to train for overtime shifts in animal control. It seemed like a simple decision at the time, but it turned out to be life-changing. I loved the idea of serving others, and here was a chance to help both animals and people. That initial opportunity turned into a full-time role as an animal warden, and one role led to another, each one building on the last. Today, as the CEO of Operation Kindness in North Texas, I realize just how much that single opportunity shaped my path and brought me to where I am today.

When I joined Operation Kindness in 2021, I stepped into an organization with a long history of success. For nearly 50 years, we had been known for placing 4,000 to 5,000 animals annually through adoptions—a remarkable achievement. But as impressive as those numbers were, I quickly realized we were only scratching the surface of what we could accomplish.

The organization had been inwardly focused, prioritizing adoptions over other opportunities to impact animal welfare. While adoptions are critical, they represent just one part of the solution. We weren't addressing upstream challenges—preventing animals from needing shelter intervention in the first place.

With the support of an amazing team, we began shifting our focus outward. We developed programs that brought services directly into the community, including spay/neuter clinics, vaccination drives, and outreach initiatives designed to keep pets in their homes. Last year alone, we impacted 46,000 animals—nearly 10 times the number of annual adoptions we once celebrated. That's the power of looking beyond what's comfortable and asking, "*What more can we do?*"

This transformation wasn't easy. Change is hard, especially when it challenges long-standing traditions. But my team stepped up. They embraced the new vision and together we've seen the tangible difference our work has made in the community. Watching them grow and thrive alongside the organization has been one of the most rewarding parts of this journey.

Building a Culture That Thrives

One of the things I'm most proud of is the culture we've built at Operation Kindness. While many organizations in our field are struggling with staff shortages, we, at the time of this writing, have 190 positions and only five vacancies. That doesn't happen by accident. It's the result of intentional leadership and a shared commitment to fostering an environment where people feel valued.

I've spent over two decades in this field, much of it in government work, where red tape often felt like shackles. Titles couldn't be changed, office spaces were assigned based on rigid hierarchies, and bureaucracy limited resources. These challenges shaped me as a leader, and when I transitioned to nonprofit work, I quickly realized just how different—and liberating—it could be. In nonprofit, I learned that things I once dismissed, like where someone's office was or their title, mattered to people. It took time to adjust, but I understood that if something was important to my staff, it needed to be important to me too.

Culture isn't just about making people feel good; it's about making them feel heard. I can't always say yes to every idea, but I make a point of explaining why. When people feel heard, they're more likely to stay engaged and keep contributing.

Balancing the Heart and the Head

Animal welfare is a deeply emotional field, and that passion is what draws so many of us to it. But emotions alone aren't enough to lead effectively. I've seen decisions made based on feelings rather than facts, and while those choices might feel right in the moment, they don't always have the greatest impact.

That's where data comes in. At Operation Kindness, we pair compassion with strategy. We analyze the numbers, track outcomes, and use that information to guide our decisions. It's easy to get wrapped up in the story of one animal—and those stories matter. But when faced with the choice between helping one animal or helping ten, I'll choose the ten every time.

Data also allows us to measure success and identify areas for improvement. We even track customer service metrics, such as the number of visitors who ultimately leave with an adopted pet. These insights ensure we're not just working hard but working smart.

Strong leadership requires balance not just between the heart and the head, but also between personal resilience and external pressures. If I could offer new leaders one piece of advice, it would be this: Don't take everything so personally. That's easier said than done, especially in an emotionally charged field. People will criticize decisions, question motives, and sometimes even attack personally. It's hard not to let that get under your skin, but staying focused on the bigger picture is essential as a leader.

Another key lesson? Celebrate progress, even when challenges seem overwhelming. I often tell my team, "we're not just trying to get through the day, we're trying to win the day."

Focusing on small, daily victories builds the momentum that leads to bigger successes over time.

Protecting the Future of our Field

Sadly, one of my biggest concerns is that good leaders are leaving the field, worn down by the emotional toll and constant scrutiny. If we push out the very people who can drive change, we risk losing the progress we've fought so hard to achieve. There aren't endless replacements waiting in the wings—we need to support and cultivate leaders who understand how to balance compassion with strategy and have the resilience to keep moving forward.

Sustaining progress means creating a culture that values both people and animals. When I think about what we've achieved at Operation Kindness, I'm reminded that no one person can take credit. Every success is a team effort—staff, volunteers, donors, and partners all play a role. Leadership isn't just about making decisions; it's about empowering others to do their best work.

That's how we keep moving forward. That's how we go from simply getting through the day to winning it.

***Ed Jamison** brings a deep belief that animal welfare is as much about people as it is about pets. Under his leadership as CEO of Operation Kindness since March 2021, he has expanded the organization's reach through innovative programs, including community initiatives, shelter partnerships, interstate transport, and animal cruelty forensics. In addition, Jamison oversees a medical wing, neonatal kitten nursery, and pet food pantry—all designed to remove barriers to care and save more lives.*

Before joining Operation Kindness, Jamison served as Director of Dallas Animal Services (DAS), one of the largest and most complex municipal shelters in the country. When he arrived in 2017, Dallas was in the spotlight for its loose dog problem. Jamison was tasked with tackling public safety while improving positive outcomes for animals. He launched the "Dallas 90" campaign to create a community where all people and animals are safe, respected, and supported—no small feat, given the annual intake of over 39,000 dogs and cats.

Jamison's roots in animal welfare go back to the early 2000s in Cleveland, Ohio, where he redefined the role of animal control as Chief Animal Control Officer. His trademarked City Dogs Cleveland® adoption and volunteer programs still thrive today and have been replicated nationwide.

In addition to leading Operation Kindness, Jamison serves as Vice President of the National Animal Care & Control Association and sits on the boards of the Association of Animal Welfare Advancement and Shelter Animals Count. At home, life is full—and furry—with his dogs Gurble and Esme, a lively clowder of cats, a goldfish, three cows, six donkeys, nine goats, and a handful of loved dogs and cats.

"Anyone can be a leader, but not everyone is a changemaker. A changemaker doesn't just see the problem—they find the solution and take action."

Ellen Jefferson

From Fixing Pets to Fixing the System

I didn't become a veterinarian because I loved biology or science. In fact, I wasn't very good at either. What I did have was an unwavering passion for animals—a drive so strong that I pushed through vet school despite not fitting the traditional mold.

Like many kids who love animals, I thought becoming a veterinarian was the only career path for people who wanted to dedicate their lives to helping them. What I didn't realize then was that helping animals went beyond medical care. I could actually impact systemic change.

A Harsh Reality Check

After graduating from Virginia Tech's Virginia-Maryland College of Veterinary Medicine, I stayed in Virginia for a year before moving to Austin, Texas. I had done my undergraduate work at Trinity University in San Antonio and was drawn to Austin's energy and progressive spirit. I took a job at an emergency animal hospital, expecting to spend my career saving pets one by one.

Then my sister suggested I volunteer at the local shelter. That decision changed everything. Austin's city shelter had an 85% euthanasia rate at the time. Out of 30,000 animals that entered the shelter annually, only a fraction made it out alive. I was stunned.

I had spent my life learning how to save animals. Yet here, healthy, adoptable pets were losing their lives simply because there were too many of them.

At first, I did what I could, performing spay/neuter surgeries and treating broken bones. But what I saw next made it clear that these small, individual efforts weren't enough. The euthanasia room and surgery room where I worked were combined into one space. I would be in the middle of a life-saving surgery while, just a few feet away, another animal was being euthanized. It was devastating. It was unacceptable. And I knew I had to do something bigger.

Creating a New Solution: Founding Emancipet

I believed the key to preventing euthanasia was preventing animals from entering the shelter in the first place. That's why, in 1998, I founded Emancipet, a low-cost spay/neuter clinic in Austin, Texas, designed to reduce shelter intake before it began.

At the time, affordable veterinary care was nearly impossible to find, especially for pet owners in low-income communities. I wanted to change that. If we could help pet owners access spay/neuter services, vaccinations, and basic care, we could slow the flood of animals into the shelter system.

For nine years, Emancipet grew into a massive operation, spaying and neutering over 100,000 animals. It was making a measurable difference, but it wasn't enough. Despite our efforts, the shelter's euthanasia rate only dropped to 55%.

That's when I realized something crucial: Prevention alone wasn't solving the problem. The animals continued to arrive, and they continued to die. I had spent nearly a decade stopping the flow, but I hadn't focused on saving the ones already in the system. That's when I knew I needed to shift from prevention to intervention.

Rethinking the No-Kill Equation

Around this time, the no-kill movement was gaining momentum, and Nathan Winograd was challenging the idea that shelter overcrowding was simply a matter of "too many pets, not enough homes."

I attended one of his talks, and something resonated with me.

"It's not overpopulation if you don't have a foster program," he said. "It's not overpopulation if your adoption hours don't match intake hours."

He was right.

The shelter wasn't just overwhelmed with animals; it lacked the necessary systems to save them. That realization led me to Austin Pets Alive! (APA!), a struggling advocacy group with no staff, no building, and no clear direction. I saw its potential and stepped in as executive director in 2008, determined to make Austin a no-kill city.

APA's approach was simple but radical:

→ We didn't rescue just any animals. We focused solely on the ones slated for euthanasia.

→ We built programs that filled the gaps in the city shelter, from fostering to medical care.

→ We made sure every effort had a measurable impact.

I am proud to say that in 2011, Austin became the largest no-kill city in the nation.

Leading with Vision and Adaptability

Leadership in animal welfare isn't about maintaining the status quo. It's about constantly evolving to meet new challenges. When you're doing groundbreaking work, at some point, what you are doing becomes the new status quo. And then new problems arise. That doesn't mean past efforts failed. It simply means we must continue to evolve.

An example of this is that in Austin, the challenge is no longer euthanasia. Now it's making sure animals don't languish in kennels for months on end. APA! is challenging the status quo once again, focusing on improving the quality of life for pets in shelters and expanding our impact beyond Austin.

A Leadership Philosophy Rooted in Action

I consider myself a *"doer,"* but I've learned that being too hands-on can sometimes stifle growth in others. The best teams excel when the goal is clear and everyone understands their role in achieving it. That's why my greatest leadership challenge—and responsibility—has been mentoring others to take ownership, build confidence, and become the next generation of changemakers.

There are plenty of ways to be a leader. You can take a job or manage a team. However, we need more people who don't just see the problem; they see the solution and take action. That, to me, is how real change happens.

If you're stepping into animal welfare leadership, here are a few things that should be top of mind:

→ **Have a vision.** People need to know where you're headed. It builds trust and direction.

→ **Be accessible.** Your team should feel they can reach you and be heard.

→ **Measure what matters.** Don't assume you're making a difference. Track your impact with real data. Data tells the story of where you are and what you are succeeding at doing.

→ **Keep evolving.** Solving one problem doesn't mean there won't be other problems to follow. Stay adaptable. And when those new problems arise, be ready to pivot and continue making societal changes that benefit animals.

Most importantly, future leaders need to step up, take risks, and turn ideas into action. Animal welfare doesn't just need managers. It needs visionaries, problem-solvers, and doers. Anyone can be a leader, but not everyone is a changemaker. A changemaker doesn't just see the problem; they find the solution and take action. The future of the animal welfare field depends on finding leaders willing to lead with purpose and passion.

***Ellen Jefferson, D.V.M.**, President & CEO of Austin Pets Alive & American Pets Alive!, is a pioneering leader whose mission has reshaped animal welfare nationally. After earning her veterinary degree in 1997,* *she founded EmanciPET two years later—a low-cost spay/neuter clinic to combat Austin's high shelter euthanasia rates. In 2008, she took the helm of Austin Pets Alive! (APA!), previously a grassroots volunteer group, and led the charge to make Austin the largest no-kill city in the United States. Under her leadership, APA! has saved over 120,000 animals regionally, achieving a live-release rate of more than 95%.*

In 2010, Dr. Jefferson launched American Pets Alive! (AmPA!), extending APA!'s lifesaving programs nationwide and providing training to hundreds of animal welfare professionals. In 2020, she spearheaded the Human Animal Support Services (HASS) initiative, a groundbreaking model supporting the human-animal bond, now adopted by over 400 organizations across the U.S. and Canada.

Her influence extends beyond program-building: Dr. Jefferson is actively engaged in shaping national policy and strategy through the Executive Team of the HASS Project, the Pedigree Foundation Shelter Advisory Council, and the Mars State of Pet Homelessness Index Board. Among her accolades are being the inaugural recipient of the Avanzino Leadership Award and receiving the Maddie's Fund Inaugural Hero Award. In recognition of her profound impact on animals and the community, the City of Austin declared November 5 "Ellen Jefferson Day" in 2016.

A national thought leader, Dr. Jefferson continues pursuing systems-level change in sheltering through data-driven strategies and humane innovation.

"Leadership often means taking risks others won't take, and believing in people before they believe in themselves."

Gina Knepp

Three Hard-Won Lessons: The Need for Courage, Trust, and Perspective

Lesson 1: Let Criticism Sharpen You, Not Break You

Leadership in animal welfare often means standing in the fire, making tough decisions, facing public scrutiny, and carrying the weight of outcomes not everyone will understand. You learn quickly that you'll never make everyone happy. Activists will sometimes oppose your choices. Social media can erupt with criticism so loud it drowns out everything else. But this work isn't a popularity contest; it's hard, relentless, and deeply important.

From 2010 to 2019, I served as Shelter Director for the City of Sacramento's Front Street Animal Shelter. In 2014, I went through one of the darkest chapters of my professional life. Public records requests flooded in. I was vilified online. There were calls for my termination. The pressure was unbearable, and I came dangerously close to breaking. It affected my team. It shattered volunteer morale. "Painful" doesn't even begin to describe it.

What had happened was that the staff's notes about animals—particularly behavioral observations—could have been clearer. And my critics had a point. Sometimes, staff put in only two sentences on an animal's intake, behavior, and medical notes when it really needed more. The notes weren't as clear, objective, or detailed as they needed to be. That vulnerability gave fuel to our critics.

In the middle of that chaos, I had to ask myself a hard question: Was there anything in this storm I could actually control? The answer turned out to be yes—and it started with looking inward.

It was important to learn how much I needed to "clean my side of the street." That moment changed everything about how we handled documentation. We retrained our team and restructured how we documented care. It didn't fix everything, but it made us better.

Looking back, I wish I had known one simple truth: *This too shall pass.* Surviving that moment taught me more than I ever expected about resilience.

It also gave me a strategy I still use today.

When the noise gets loud, I've learned to listen for the lesson. In every wave of criticism, there may be a kernel of truth. Find it. Own it. Fix it. It's easy to dismiss your critics as unhinged, but sometimes, their sharpest barbs reveal real blind spots.

Criticism will come. Let it sharpen you, not break you. Don't ignore it; face it, and stay strong. Without courage, criticism will crush you. With it, you can face the fire, learn what you need to learn—and keep going.

Lesson 2: Trust Your Gut: Invest in People Others Overlook

Over the years, I've had the privilege of working alongside many incredibly talented people. In two remarkable cases, I was fortunate to recognize a rare, almost preternatural potential—hidden beneath inexperience and overlooked by their peers. These individuals were young, unproven, and, in the beginning, not easily accepted. But I saw something extraordinary in them.

Unconcerned with popular opinion, I made the deliberate choice to champion their growth. I challenged them to rise above the noise, to silence the skeptics, and to chart a course guided by their own North Star—no matter how turbulent the path.

It wasn't easy.

Leadership often means taking risks others won't take and believing in people before they believe in themselves. At times, my decisions were questioned. For those I elevated, the journey meant enduring scrutiny and proving themselves in the face of relentless doubt.

But with time, the very peer groups that once dismissed them came to see what I had seen from the start: brilliance, drive, and a capacity for excellence far beyond the norm.

Today, I'm proud to say that both individuals have grown into exceptional leaders within our field. One now oversees one of the largest humane law enforcement teams in California—managing investigations, casework, emergency response, officer training, dispatch, and working closely with courts and law enforcement agencies. The other leads transformative advocacy efforts—designing community programs, humane education, and public pet services—all centered on the mission of keeping people and pets together.

Both began their careers at the very foundation of animal sheltering—in entry-level roles, often cleaning kennels or answering phones. What set them apart wasn't just raw talent; it was an insatiable hunger to learn and a relentless drive to make a difference.

They were simply overlooked—until someone saw their potential.

Sometimes, the path to organizational growth means swimming against the current. It's about taking bold chances on people others overlook—and trusting that with belief and support, their potential can grow into something lasting. Today, they're living proof that world-class leaders can rise from the most unassuming beginnings when given the chance to shine.

Lesson 3:
Keep Perspective, or the Work Will Break You

Our industry feels vast when you're deep in the daily work of sheltering animals—but in truth, it's quite small. Immersed in the urgency of shelter life, it can feel like we're carrying the weight of the entire pet population on our shoulders. That burden can be overwhelming.

Perspective is the anchor that keeps us from burning out.

Each year, an estimated 6.3 million dogs and cats (*source: Shelter Animals Count*) enter shelters in the U.S. Compare that to the approximately 163.5 million pets—89.7 million dogs and 73.8 million cats—living in homes across the country (*Source: The American Veterinary Medical Association*). Shelters touch only about 3.85% of that total. Just a sliver.

That sliver matters deeply, but so does the bigger picture. The truth is, most pet owners are doing a good job caring for their animals. Many pets are loved, well cared for, and thriving, and that's something worth celebrating. We've done a good job educating people about how to care for their pets. We must hold onto that truth. Every success story reminds us why we do this work—and why we can't stop now.

Without perspective, our work can feel impossible. But with it, we can stay grounded, focused, and hopeful—and continue to fight for those who need us.

***Gina Knepp** is a nationally recognized leader in animal welfare, currently serving as Senior Specialist of Outreach & Engagement at Petco Love. She leads the expansion of Petco Love Lost, a tech-driven platform helping reunite lost pets with their families faster and more often.*

Previously, Knepp spent five years at Michelson Found Animals, where she helped spark a national movement to modernize the recovery of lost pets. Her journey began at Front Street Animal Shelter in

Sacramento, California, where where she transformed a high-intake municipal shelter into a model of community engagement and innovation.

Knepp is a sought-after expert in shelter operations, volunteer engagement, and customer service. Before entering animal welfare, she managed 911 and 311 services for the City of Sacramento—an experience that continues to inform her leadership. With a rare blend of grit, heart, and vision, Knepp is transforming the way communities care for their pets.

Events
KFAST SPECIAL

"I didn't get into this for my own advancement. I didn't get into this to create an organization that would last forever. I got into this to help the cats—and when there's a conflict between those things, the cats will always win."

Bryan Kortis

Putting the Mission First: A Life Dedicated to Community Cats

I never set out to be a leader. I never cared about titles, recognition, or making a name for myself. What has always mattered most to me is the mission—helping community cats.

For over two decades, I've worked to advance Trap-Neuter-Return (TNR) and reshape the world's view and management of free-roaming cats. As co-founder of Neighborhood Cats in 1999, I've spent my career advocating for humane and effective solutions for outdoor cats. Despite our small size—we've never had more than five employees or a budget over $700,000—our work has influenced how community cats are managed nationwide and, increasingly, internationally.

People often ask how a small nonprofit gained such significant influence. The answer is simple: we took risks. Risks that could have cost me my career. Risks that could have shut down my organization. Risks that, in some cases, drew sharp criticism from within the animal welfare community itself.

But I took them because, at the end of the day, the cats always come first.

Risking Everything to Work with "The Enemy"

In the early 2000s, TNR was still a fringe concept in New York City where I lived at the time. While a handful of individual rescuers practiced it, no groups or major organizations had adopted it. Affordable spay/neuter services for feral cats were almost completely unavailable. Initially, we sought private veterinarians who had recently opened their practices, were in need of cash flow, and were willing to provide low-cost services, fixing one or two cats at a time.

New York City's municipal shelter, then known as the Center for Animal Care and Control (CACC), was euthanizing 70 to 75% of the cats that entered their doors. Their facilities were outdated, their resources were stretched thin, and they had inherited a system that was simply not designed to save animals. At the time, the local rescue community vilified them and never missed an opportunity to criticize.

But they weren't "the enemy." They were simply overwhelmed. And that's where I saw an opportunity.

Instead of working against them, we decided to work with them. We approached the shelter and proposed a partnership. Whenever an ear-tipped cat (a sign of a sterilized community cat) was impounded, we would be contacted so we could attempt to locate the caretaker and return the cat to its outdoor home.

To my surprise, they were immediately on board. They were desperate for solutions and eager for outside help. They saw this for what it was—the first step in supporting our budding TNR program.

In the first few years, this simple policy saved dozens of cats from unnecessary euthanasia. Just as importantly, it also built trust. Community cat caretakers were incentivized to do TNR, knowing their altered colony cats had a measure of protection. Plus, people began to change their views of the shelter, knowing that ear-tipped cats wouldn't automatically be put down.

But not everyone saw it that way.

At the time, many rescuers were deeply skeptical of TNR. Some strongly believed cats did not belong on the streets and should be removed entirely. Others distrusted the city shelter, worried their involvement with Neighborhood Cats masked what was still a deep hostility to cats. Our decision to work with the shelter, rather than publicly condemn them, didn't sit well with some groups.

People weren't calling us traitors, but they were questioning whether this was the right course of action. There was a risk in trusting a system that had historically failed cats. But for me, the choice was clear: we could stand outside the system and attack it, or we could work from within and change it.

We chose change. And it worked. Today, the CACC, now known as Animal Care Centers of NYC, is one of our strongest partners when it comes to protecting community cats.

Bringing TNR into the Mainstream

By the mid-2000s, TNR was gaining traction, but it still wasn't mainstream. Most national organizations were hesitant to endorse it fully, and one of the most significant barriers was the Humane Society of the United States (HSUS), now known as Humane World for Animals.

At the time, HSUS's policy on community cats was vague at best, outright hostile at worst. Many of their representatives believed cats were better off euthanized than living outdoors, even if they were fed regularly and cared for. Their stance wasn't entirely their fault. Since its introduction to the U.S. in the early 1990s, TNR had been framed by critics as "abandonment," and they were following this traditional sheltering perspective.

But I knew that if TNR was ever going to be widely accepted, we needed the backing of the major national organizations. The ASPCA, headquartered in New York City, had come around after working with us on hands-on projects, but HSUS remained an obstacle. So, we reached out. Getting a meeting with HSUS leadership was nearly impossible. But then one day, we got a call: "*Wayne*

Pacelle, HSUS's new CEO, has an hour free tomorrow in Atlanta during our annual conference. Are you attending, and can you meet with him?"

We were in New York and had no plans to be in Atlanta. But we said, *"Yes! We'll be there."*

We booked last-minute flights, landed in Atlanta the next morning, and pretended we had already been in town.

That meeting changed everything.

Soon after, HSUS rewrote its policy on community cats and funded a national tour of TNR workshops instructed by me. I wrote educational materials for their website, produced a short documentary video, and authored a guide on creating communitywide programs. This was a major breakthrough for TNR, further legitimizing it on a national scale.

Of course, not everyone was happy about it. Some claimed I had abandoned grassroots advocacy in favor of working with a big organization that didn't really have the cats' best interests at heart. I was even accused of selling out the cats in favor of gaining the national limelight. But here's the thing: I didn't care what they said or about getting credit. I cared about making progress.

Putting the Cause Over Ego

One of the best examples of this mission-first approach occurred in 2002, when we led what, at the time, was one of the largest single-site TNR projects ever conducted on Rikers Island, New York City's main jail complex. For years, the jail had been dealing with a massive cat overpopulation problem. It had even made headlines for alleged animal cruelty. In the face of all the bad publicity the authorities were facing, we convinced them to let us run a TNR program.

We coordinated with multiple groups, including the ASPCA and the city shelter, to spay and neuter, and return nearly 300 cats. It was a success, and we were ready to share the news with the media. Then, right before press day, the entire collaboration nearly collapsed.

Not over the cats or the work, but over logo placement on the press release. One group demanded that their name and logo be listed first. Another fought back. Suddenly, the focus shifted from the cats to who was getting credit for the project.

I stepped in and said, *"Put Neighborhood Cats last."*

That ended the argument. Press day and the rest of the project moved forward. National attention was brought to TNR, greatly raising awareness of the method. Because at the end of the day, this work isn't about getting recognition. It's about saving lives.

Creating Mission-Driven Leadership

The animal welfare field can sometimes have a short attention span. For a while, TNR was the "hot topic." Then, focus shifted to the human-animal bond, and then to access to veterinary care. Now, the biggest funding goes toward diversion programs. But I haven't changed my focus. I'm still working on community cats because that's where the need remains. Leadership isn't about chasing trends. It's about staying committed to what matters, even when it's no longer in the spotlight.

So, if I could give one piece of advice to the next generation of animal welfare leaders, it would be this: Forget about titles. Forget about credit. Forget about personal recognition. Do the work to the best of your ability. If you do that, everything else—support, funding, influence—will follow.

Remember, leadership isn't about being the loudest voice in the room. It's about being the most persistent. It's about putting the mission first, even when no one is watching. It's about being willing to take the hits when your choices aren't popular because you know they're right.

It's also about playing the long game. Change doesn't happen overnight. It doesn't happen in one grant cycle or one strategic plan. If you want to make a real impact, you have to be in this for the long haul.

So don't be discouraged when the industry shifts its focus. Stay the course. Continue doing the work that needs to be done, even when funding fades, trends change, and attention moves elsewhere.

Because in the end, it's not about us.

It's about the cats.

***Bryan Kortis, J.D.,** is a pioneering leader in humane community cat management, whose work has helped transform how cities nationwide approach TNR. As co-founder and National Programs Director for Neighborhood Cats, Kortis established one of America's most effective community cat organizations. Since starting his TNR work in 1999, he has personally trapped thousands of cats, first on Manhattan's Upper West Side and more recently during the aftermath of wildfires in Maui, helping shape best practices and policy acceptance.*

From 2010 through 2015, Kortis served as grants manager at PetSmart Charities, overseeing millions in funding for TNR and community cat initiatives. He has authored and co-authored several cornerstone publications, including the "Neighborhood Cats TNR Handbook," "Community TNR: Tactics & Tools,"and "The Return-to-Field Handbook." He also regularly presents workshops and advanced webinars on strategic, targeted TNR implementation as well as on advocacy, trapping techniques, and community cat care.

Many other ground-level innovations in TNR have been developed by Kortis and Neighborhood Cats. They were the first to introduce the concept of mass trapping (the TNR of an entire colony at once), as well as using traps to hold and care for TNR cats. With Tomahawk Live Trap, they co-designed the first commercially available drop trap, as well as a host of other popular trapping equipment.

Kortis' multifaceted experience, as a former attorney turned cat advocate, gives him unique insight into creating effective nonprofit-government partnerships. He continues to support Neighborhood Cats' programs in New York City, New Jersey, and Hawai'i, while providing consultation and training to municipalities, shelters, and grassroots groups across the U.S. seeking durable, data-driven community cat solutions.

"Culture starts with leaders, but it lives in every corner of an organization."

Laura Maloney

Hurricane Katrina: Leading Through the Eye of the Storm

When Hurricane Katrina devastated New Orleans in 2005, it altered lives forever, dismantling homes, communities, and an entire way of life. At the Louisiana SPCA, in New Orleans, our staff lost not only their homes and vehicles but, in some cases, friends and family to death, illness, or displacement. And our shelter? Gone. We had no physical location to operate from, but the need didn't disappear. Thousands of animals and their people needed help.

There was no rulebook for what to do. Neither New Orleans nor the nation had faced such a disaster. We were in crisis. While we had a well-tested evacuation plan, what held us together in the days that followed wasn't a plan on paper. It was our culture: the trust we had in one another, the cohesion of our team, and the belief that if we supported each other, we could face anything.

Culture as a Lifeline

In those early days, our 15-person team stayed at my father's house in Baton Rouge. Several weeks in, we purchased a house near Lamar Dixon (an equine center)—what became our initial rescue center—so our team could shower, grab a few hours of sleep, and regroup. Taking care of each other mattered. Taking care of one another is what enabled us to care for thousands of animals and endure the two years that followed, operating from a makeshift shelter, washing dishes in a tent, and raising the funds to build anew.

People flew in from all over the country, eager to lend a hand. Their presence was both a blessing and overwhelming. With no central plan in place, cohesion mattered more than hierarchy. Volunteers arrived with different philosophies and approaches, but our culture of respect and purpose gave us the ability to carry forward.

We didn't have a central command structure, but we had urgency and compassion. Quick decision-making and adaptability were possible because leadership was distributed, not centralized. Everyone had a role, a responsibility, and the trust to act. That shared empowerment created cohesion out of chaos.

From Chaos to Cohesion

As I moved between the streets of New Orleans, the Emergency Operations Center where I became a regular participant, and the horse barns that served as our base, we built a rhythm of care—person to person, house by house, stall by stall, with dogs, cats, and other small pets filling the stalls where horses once stood. The work was beyond exhausting, but our shared respect and culture gave it structure.

The toll on our people was staggering. The Society for Industrial and Organizational Psychology studied our team for two years and assessed individual stress levels. A score of 300 was considered an extreme level of stress. Our staff averaged 1,300! By those standards, they should have all dropped dead from heart attacks months earlier. That they didn't is a testament to their commitment and to the culture of care, trust, and cohesion that kept us standing.

People were empowered to act without micromanaging. We stayed deeply human with one another, holding space for grief, exhaustion, and fear, while also nurturing resilience and calm.

I have always believed that a shelter's team is the true instrument of change. When we take care of the people, they take care of the mission. And they did. Our culture of trust, empowerment, and shared leadership was the real lifeline.

Shifting Leadership, Strengthening Culture

Disaster changed me, as it did our team. Before Katrina, I was (and still am) a consensus builder, drawing on the strengths of each person regardless of role. But I learned that in a disaster, consensus is not always effective. In the middle of chaos, when decisions had to be made in minutes and lives depended on them, I could step forward and give clear direction, but the cost to me was high. Acting against my natural style meant carrying not just the weight of the choices, but the strain of leading in a way that did not come naturally.

I had another chance to test this balance during Hurricane Sandy, when I was Chief Operating Officer at The Humane Society of the United States (currently known as Humane World for Animals). By then, I could move more fluidly between consensus and direction—drawing on group wisdom when time allowed, and issuing direct instructions when urgency required it. It was a different kind of storm, but the leadership muscles I had built during Katrina gave me the confidence to navigate both approaches and manage the benefits of each.

During Katrina, with thousands of volunteers, dozens of humane societies on the ground, and no way to communicate beyond daily huddles at Lamar Dixon, my instinct for consensus was stretched to its limits. By the time Hurricane Sandy hit, cell phones had restored basic communication, making the work less taxing and allowing me to see my leadership style shift. I had become more comfortable striking a balance between consensus and direction.

Lessons That Last

What Katrina clarified for me was that leading in crisis and leading in growth require the same fundamentals: trust, alignment, clarity, and care. These are not simply strategies; they are cultural foundations.

Later, in national and executive roles across the nonprofit landscape, I saw the same truth play out. Whether working with executive teams to shape organization-wide strategies, helping staff manage burnout, guiding boards through conflict, or supporting leaders as they found their footing, culture proved to be the differentiator. You can give two organizations the same strategic plan, yet each will execute it differently. Culture is the real competitive advantage.

When people feel seen, supported, and trusted, they find commonality even in the most challenging circumstances. Culture provides clarity, a framework for managing conflict, and a stake in the ground for how people engage and perform. It is the engine of a healthy organization.

Leadership as a Cultural Practice

Leadership is never about a title or being the loudest voice in the room; it's about being the most effective leader. It is about cultivating culture every day—showing up with empathy, creating clarity in uncertainty, and helping others be seen and to shine.

Tone starts at the top, and it is felt in every corner of an organization. From how we treat each other in meetings to how we support staff in crisis, leaders set the culture by what they do, not just what they say.

Katrina was the storm that tested us beyond imagination, but it also revealed the strength that would guide us forever: culture is the lifeline. It kept us together when we had no shelter, no offices, and no road map. It shaped how I led through Sandy and beyond. And it continues to remind me—and hopefully reminds others—that even in the darkest storms, trust, compassion, and shared purpose can carry us through. That is the legacy Katrina left with me, and it is the lesson I carry into every room, every board meeting, and every team I support today.

***Laura Maloney** is a leadership and team coach with nearly three decades of executive experience spanning animal welfare, wildlife conservation, and nonprofit management. She is best known for her tenure as CEO of the Louisiana SPCA, where she led the organization* *before, during, and after Hurricane Katrina. In the aftermath of the storm, with the shelter destroyed and her staff displaced, Maloney played a critical leadership role in one of the most complex animal rescue and recovery efforts in U.S. history. Her ability to rally staff, volunteers, and national organizations in the face of chaos and to share leadership has become a defining example of leadership in crisis.*

Following Katrina, Maloney expanded her leadership footprint nationally and globally. She served as Chief Operating Officer of The Humane Society of the United States (currently known as Humane World for Animals), overseeing key operational areas, including five accredited wildlife and equine centers across the U.S., as well as animal rescue. She later served as Chief Operating Officer of Panthera, a conservation organization working in more than 47 countries to protect wild cats and their habitats. Across these roles, she became recognized for balancing strategic vision with operational execution, collaborating with teams who managed challenging logistics while navigating complex cultural and political landscapes.

Today, as a strategic consultant and nonprofit leader, Maloney partners with executives, boards, and staff across sectors to strengthen organizational health, cultivate adaptive leadership, and drive overall effectiveness. She brings a unique blend of lived crisis experience, national and global perspective, and a deeply human-centered approach to every engagement. Her work is grounded in the belief that leaders set the tone, but culture lives in every corner of an organization—and when people feel seen, supported, and trusted, they are empowered to achieve extraordinary results.

"My father always told me, 'Don't be afraid of change—you can always change again.' And that's been true my whole life."

Nancy May

From Part-Time Plans to Full-Time Purpose

After more than 35 years in the banking industry as a trust officer and wealth advisor, I thought I was ready for retirement. Six months in, however, I realized I still had more to give. I loved the structure, the people, the challenges—and I missed the work.

Several nonprofits reached out about part-time opportunities, but many would have required me to recuse myself due to other foundation board affiliations. The San Antonio Humane Society (SAHS), however, stood out. None of my foundations had ties to animal welfare, and I had always loved animals—even though I wasn't allowed to have them growing up. Now, I could make up for lost time.

I started in donor relations on a part-time basis. That was all I wanted. However, when the executive director left, the board asked if I would serve as the interim executive director. I agreed, still intending to keep things temporary and part-time. But within a few months, I realized I was enjoying the work and felt I was making a difference. The board appreciated the impact I was having, even if they didn't always love what I had to say. They offered me a full-time job, and I accepted. That was in 2009. I eventually became the Interim President and CEO in 2011 and was officially named President and CEO in 2012.

I didn't dream I would be here 15 years.

Putting My Skills to Work

Transitioning from banking to animal welfare was more natural than people might expect. Nonprofits may not be profit-driven, but they still need to run efficiently and transparently. My background in finance enabled me to thoroughly review the books, clean up neglected records, and establish fiscal stability within the organization. I even found a stack of unexecuted oil and gas leases under a desk—a detail that reminded me of the value of broad, transferable skills.

When I began, we had 47 employees. Today, we have 93. I had supervised teams in banking, but never for this many people at once. Communication became my most important tool. I leaned heavily on organization, discipline, and a willingness to listen to staff and observe before acting. My father always told me, *"Don't be afraid of change. You can always change again."*

That flexibility has served me well, especially in times of crisis.

One of those moments was during the COVID-19 pandemic. As an essential business with live animals, we couldn't shut down. We adapted quickly: drive-through vaccinations, no-contact adoptions, and virtual meet-and-greets. Our staff wore full protective gear to safely deliver pets to new families. It was challenging, but we never stopped serving the community. At the same time, we were building our 17,000 sq. ft. medical building—a huge project that required partnership, transparency, and constant communication. The staff really stepped up in a big way to keep the mission going.

I have always believed in treating staff like partners. So, when designing our new 17,000 sq. ft. medical facility, I included our medical team in the process. I traveled across the U.S. to see what others were doing well and brought in staff to give feedback. Their insights helped shape a more effective, functional facility.

From Novice to Advocate

When I first arrived, I had no experience in animal welfare. Some people even questioned whether I was right for the role. But I engaged those individuals, asked them to teach me, and in turn, I shared my skills with them. We grew together. I've remained lifelong friends with most everybody. Some of the skeptics became my greatest supporters—and even my friends. Some of the people we've had to let go still come to our events and give me big hugs. That surprises me but also makes me happy. It means we're treating people with respect and kindness.

What do I believe makes a strong leader? Listening. Organization. Discipline. And above all, relationship building. I value people. I value animals. I believe the best outcomes come when you combine both. My leadership philosophy has always been to work alongside people, not above them. That's how trust is built—with donors, staff, volunteers, and the broader community.

I never imagined I would end up in animal welfare. But looking back, every path I took prepared me for this work. I get to love animals and make a difference, and I get to help people while doing it.

That, to me, is the essence of leadership—making a difference in people's lives.

***Nancy May** is the President and CEO of the SAHS in San Antonio, Texas, a position she has held since 2012. With a deep commitment to animal welfare and community engagement, May has guided the organization through years of growth, innovation, and increased impact. Under her leadership, SAHS has strengthened its programs, achieved fiscal stability, and adopted a donor-centered approach that prioritizes meaningful relationships and philanthropy.*

Before becoming CEO, May served as Planned Gifts and Donor Relations Officer for SAHS, building lasting connections with supporters and raising awareness about legacy giving. Her earlier career spans more than three decades in banking and wealth management, including senior leadership roles at Broadway National Bank, U.S. Trust, and Bexar County National Bank, where she specialized in managing trusts, foundations, and estate relationships.

A proud graduate of Texas State University with a degree in Education and Mathematics, May is also a Certified Trust Financial Advisor. She is a respected community leader, serving on numerous boards, including The Genevieve and Ward Orsinger Foundation, The Charles Baumberger Endowment, The Science Mill, and ABODE. Her work has earned her several accolades, including the San Antonio Business Journal's Women's Leadership Award and the North Star Award from the San Antonio Women's Chamber of Commerce.

"Leadership is not reserved for the few; it lives in all of us."

Esther Mechler

From Anger to Action: How One Cat Sparked a National Spay/Neuter Movement

I got into this field quite by accident—or perhaps it was fate. It was 1990, and I had gone to the animal control shelter in Bridgeport, Connecticut. There, among the cages, sat a serene, beautiful cat whom I immediately named Buddha. He had a calm presence about him, a quiet grace. I already had too many cats at home, but I couldn't bear the thought of him not finding a family. I asked the shelter staff to hold him for two weeks while I searched for a home.

When I returned, Buddha was gone. Euthanized.

I was devastated. And I was angry. How could such a beautiful, friendly cat not be given a chance? That anger turned into a burning sense of purpose. I realized that if Buddha had never been born, he wouldn't have suffered that fate. The deeper issue wasn't just finding homes for animals; it was preventing unwanted litters in the first place.

Rethinking Spay/Neuter Timing

Cats outproduce humans by 45 to 1, dogs by 15 to 1. There is simply no way to find good homes for them all unless we reduce the baseline number of births. And timing matters. For years, the standard advice was to spay or neuter cats at six months of age, but by then, it's often too late. Cats can go into heat and become pregnant as early as four months old. That two-month gap has led to countless litters being born simply because we waited too long. The shelters were overflowing.

In 2016, my nonprofit, Marian's Dream, convened a task force of veterinarians at the North American Veterinary Conference to tackle this very issue. (I named Marian's Dream in honor of my sister, who died young. I wanted to do something meaningful in her memory—something that reflected her kindness and the good she brought into the world.) The result was a new veterinary consensus: spay or neuter cats by five months of age, or before their first heat. We called the campaign "Feline Fix by Five."

That small shift—just one month earlier—meant the difference between preventing a litter or not. And it's backed by science. Kittens recover quickly from surgery, the risks are lower, and the benefits are enormous. Within a year, every major national veterinary organization—the American Veterinary Medical Association, the American Animal Hospital Association, the American Association of Feline Practitioners, and the Association of Shelter Veterinarians—endorsed the recommendation.

The Power of Persistence

Now we faced the challenge of getting individual veterinarians on board. But I believe in the power of persistence. I started small. I asked my own veterinarian if he would offer discounted spay/neuter surgeries to the people I referred to him. He said yes. Encouraged, I began calling other shelters and veterinarians around my state, then around the country. To my surprise, many were already offering discounted services. They just needed help connecting with the public.

I helped build those connections. Within three years, we had over 8,000 veterinarians participating and were receiving tens of thousands of calls per month through a toll-free number. That network eventually became SPAY/USA, connecting thousands of pet owners with affordable options for over two decades.

Over the next two decades, I watched a movement grow. From mobile clinics to voucher programs, from pop-up events to high-volume spay/neuter clinics, the momentum built. By 2010, U.S. shelter euthanasia numbers dropped from 12 million to 3 million annually. That progress was made possible by countless hard-working people who shared a vision and were willing to roll up their sleeves.

Although SPAY/USA played a vital role in connecting people to affordable spay/neuter for decades, its visibility declined after I stepped away. In 2015, I founded the United Spay Alliance, a new nonprofit organization that builds upon and expands the mission with a more localized, state-by-state approach. Today, United Spay Alliance leads efforts to promote Fix by Five, addresses the national veterinary shortage, supports training through wet labs, and shares knowledge through podcasts and collaborations. I may have retired from SPAY/USA, but United Spay Alliance remains my active focus—and I'm proud of the incredible team carrying this work forward.

Today, I continue to advocate for better policies, increased awareness, and support for veterinarians who commit to early spaying and neutering of pets. I never set out to be a leader. I just saw a problem no one else seemed to be tackling, and I couldn't ignore it.

Five Things I Have Learned

Leadership is not about titles or visibility. It's about action. Here are five things I've learned in over 50 years of animal welfare work:

1. **Connect Where You Can**: Seek kindred spirits. This work is too hard to do alone.

2. **Stay Focused**: There are many worthy causes in animal welfare, but to make a difference, choose one and become an expert in it. I focused on spay/neuter. Others, like Allie Phillips, an attorney, author, educator, and advocate, chose to protect pets in domestic violence situations. Respect your path and support others on theirs.

3. Give Credit Where Credit Is Due: Nothing is more demoralizing than watching someone take credit for work they didn't do. Don't be that person. Recognize and celebrate others.

4. Don't Sell Out: It's tempting to shift your mission to attract funding, but that can sabotage your integrity. Stay true to your goals.

5. Never Give Up: There will be times when you need to pause—but never stop. Rest, regroup, and keep going.

I never wanted to lead a national movement. I just didn't want another Buddha to die. That one cat changed my life, and helped change the lives of millions more.

Leadership is not reserved for the few; it lives in all of us. It emerges when you take action despite doubt; when you stay the course through frustration; and when you inspire others by simply doing the work. You don't need to be at the front of the room to lead; sometimes, leadership is making the phone call no one else will, holding the line when it's tough, or daring to believe change is possible.

True leadership grows from compassion, courage, and commitment—and if you have those, you're already leading.

***Esther Mechler** has been at the forefront of humane strategies to reduce pet overpopulation for more than three decades. Armed with degrees in Psychology and Education from Bates College in Lewiston, Maine, and the University of Rochester in New York, Mechler initially advanced her career in guidance counseling and law school admissions. But in 1990, driven by the plight of adoptable cats at her local shelter, she pivoted her career entirely, founding SPAY/USA, a pioneering program that brought together veterinarians and clinics nationwide to make affordable, accessible spay/neuter services easier for pet owners to find.*

Within three years, SPAY/USA grew into a national network of more than 8,000 affordable clinics and programs, which eventually became part of the North Shore Animal League. In the early 2000s, grassroots leaders across the country inspired her to expand beyond referral networks toward proactive engagement. So, in 2015 Mechler founded United Spay Alliance, with a mission to ensure every cat and dog has a chance for a loving home.

Mechler is also the driving force behind Feline Fix by Five, an influential campaign launched in the late 1990s, advocating feline spay/neuter by five months of age. This initiative has since garnered broad endorsements from leading veterinary organizations, including the American Veterinary Medical Association, American Animal Hospital Association, American Association of Feline Practitioners, and Association of Shelter Veterinarians, as well as numerous state veterinary associations.

As founder of both SPAY/USA and United Spay Alliance, Mechler's leadership has shaped both policy and community education. She continues to lend her voice and expertise to initiatives that reshape how animal welfare is practiced, ensuring that compassion is rooted in impactful, scalable action.

"Because in the end, leadership is less about having the answers, and more about creating space for what's possible."

Shelly Moore

Creating Space for What's Possible

I never set out to become an executive director. Like many in animal welfare, I stumbled into it. My degree was in criminology, and I originally dreamed of becoming a forensic investigator. But one spontaneous visit to an animal shelter soon after I graduated from college changed everything. I got a part-time job working in the kennels—and things just started to unfold from there.

A short time into this new career, I was encouraged to apply for an animal control officer position. I didn't know what it entailed, but I was young and open to it. A year and a half later, I was moved into cruelty investigations. Suddenly, my degree made sense. In my early twenties, introverted and shy, I was knocking on doors, seizing animals, and testifying in court. I had to transform myself to do that job and be willing to talk with people. Eventually, I was promoted to director of investigations, and led a team, prepped cases for court, and handled the worst of the worst. I felt I found my calling.

Then came the change I didn't see coming: a new director was hired who decided to dismantle the cruelty unit. I strongly objected, but he just told me to start a humane education program. I had no children, no background in humane education, and no clue where to begin. But I'm resourceful. I joined educator groups, researched programs, and started building something new.

And then one day, I asked him if we could discuss the program's direction to ensure we were aligned. He didn't even look up from his computer. He just said, *"Let me finish this game of bridge."* That moment changed everything for me. As I walked down the hall, I thought, *"If he can run an animal shelter, so can I."*

That's often where leadership starts—not with expertise, but with the recognition that you can do something new or better.

Finding My Footing

I spent ten years in government and union work, but I knew this wasn't the path for me. I started applying for nonprofit executive director jobs. Then, I bumped into board members from the humane society in my hometown of Hagerstown, Maryland. They were hiring a new executive director. I applied and got the job.

I had never been an executive director before, but I had experience in leadership. It was a small organization, so I helped with cleaning kennels, answering phones, performing euthanasia, and assisting with adoptions. The system there wasn't totally broken, but the processes were outdated. I didn't know yet what I needed to know to lead, but I could see the possibilities. Thankfully, I had a supportive board that saw the possibilities in me and helped me grow. Over the course of six years, we implemented major changes and launched a capital campaign to construct a new facility.

That marked the beginning of a defining thread in my career: building new animal shelters.

Fixing the Culture First

As it turned out, my husband landed a job in South Carolina while I was still in Maryland. I wasn't sure what was next. Then Asheville Humane Society in Asheville, North Carolina, came calling. They wanted someone to lead their building project, and it was close to where my husband was working.

When I arrived, I quickly realized the organization wasn't ready to grow. It needed stabilizing. There had been significant turnover, particularly at the executive level, and the previous director had left the organization disorganized. While most people don't love dysfunction, I discovered that, for some reason, I liked addressing the chaos and putting systems in place. That's when I realized I'm a fixer. I understood that my strength was identifying what was possible and figuring out how to get us there.

During my ten years in Asheville, we ended our contract with law enforcement to do field enforcement. Instead, we focused on sheltering. We passed a mandatory spay/neuter law, something I helped shape, and partnered with the Humane Alliance (now part of the ASPCA), which gave the community access to high-quality, high-volume surgeries. Eventually, we became one of the ASPCA's "Orange Communities," one of a few cities in the U.S. that received funding, training, and support to pilot new, progressive approaches to animal welfare. It was a turning point for us. We shifted from siloed, judgmental sheltering to community-centered care.

While in Asheville, we built two buildings. One of them housed a veterinary technician program for the local community college, which included classrooms, labs, and surgery space. At the time, very few shelters integrated education and sheltering in that manner. It was innovative and exciting to see the direction we were moving in. The second building was a new shelter, designed primarily as an adoption center, creating a more welcoming and accessible space for both the public and the animals.

Leadership sometimes means slowing down to build the right foundation before moving forward.

The Charlotte Chapter

Around that time, I began hearing rumblings about the Humane Society of Charlotte. They were experiencing internal dysfunction, founder syndrome, and a board made up of family and friends. Things eventually came to a head: new board members sued the organization for violating its own bylaws. A judge placed the shelter in receivership and mandated a full reset—new bylaws, a new board, a clean slate.

Between 2005 and 2010, the organization underwent six executive director changes. During this time, a recruiter kept calling me for the executive director position. I kept saying no. I was in the middle of the second building project in Asheville and didn't want to leave until it was done. But I couldn't shake the thought of working in Charlotte. I couldn't sleep. All I could do was picture myself in Charlotte and the possibilities there.

Eventually, I said yes to Charlotte.

On my first day at work, I walked into an organization with 26 staff, a $400,000 deficit on a $2.6 million budget, and an IRS auditor waiting in my conference room. That was my welcome to Charlotte.

But that wasn't the only issue. As I settled in, I realized our entire identity was based on what we didn't do: we *didn't* euthanize animals. That was our only story. And it wasn't enough. I told the board, *"We have a problem. If the only story we're telling is what we don't do, we're not building trust or connection in the community."*

So, before we could do anything else, we reframed our narrative. We focused on what we *did* for the community—our services, our impact, and our values. We dropped the "no-kill" language and emphasized solutions, transparency, and community.

Over the next decade, we rebuilt the culture. Some staff members couldn't or wouldn't change, resulting in some turnover. But we brought in new leaders who helped implement open adoptions and usher in a new era of inclusive sheltering. Today, we have a strong team, solid financials, a community-focused mission, and a culture I'm proud of. And yes, we built another building—my fourth.

Strong leadership sometimes involves reframing narratives to move your team and your community forward.

Contributing Beyond Our Walls

As our internal culture grew stronger, so did our commitment to the field as a whole. I've always believed that leadership doesn't stop at your organization's edge. It involves lifting others, sharing what works, and contributing to collective progress.

At The Humane Society of Charlotte, we've become a learning organization. We encourage staff to serve on national and state committees, present at conferences, and take on leadership roles in the field. Internally, we employ a formal, collaborative approach to major decisions, such as our weekly pathway planning process for animals in our care. This fosters transparency, builds shared accountability, and ensures our choices align with both mission and capacity.

We also welcome animal welfare professionals from across the country who want to tour our shelter, shadow our team, or learn about our practices. We believe in contributing to the larger movement, not just our own community. If our experience can help others grow, we're happy to share it. Because you can't change the field if you're not willing to share what you've learned.

So, to emerging leaders, here's what I've learned along the way:

→ **Own your leadership style.** Be transparent, be present, and most of all, be human.

→ **Invest in your team.** Create space for learning, growth, and the occasional misstep. That's how people develop.

→ **Tell your story.** Don't let your community define you by what you *don't* do. Share who you are, what you stand for, and why it matters.

→ **Shape your board.** Recruit with purpose. Build real relationships. Ensure your board is aligned with the mission, not just the budget.

→ **Take calculated risks.** Innovation doesn't come from playing it safe. Try new things—and learn from what doesn't work.

→ **Show up.** Especially when it's hard. Leadership starts at the front, not from behind a desk.

→ **Stay humble.** Share the credit, own your mistakes, and make room for others to shine.

→ **Know the difference between management and leadership.** Both are essential. Learn the skills for both and when to use them.

After 40 years in the field, I still love this work. Not because it's easy, but because I still see the potential—in people, organizations, and the future of this field. I've always been a fixer. But what I've learned is that leadership isn't just about fixing what's broken. It's about building what's possible.

__Shelly Moore__ is a visionary leader whose four-decade career in animal welfare has transformed communities, elevated organizations, and inspired a new generation of leaders. As President & CEO of the Humane Society of Charlotte (HSC) in Charlotte, North Carolina, she is known not only for her strategic mind and relentless energy but also for leading with heart, humor, and humanity.

Before joining HSC, Moore served as CEO of Asheville Humane Society in Asheville, North Carolina, for ten years and held leadership roles at the Humane Society of Washington County in Hagerstown, Maryland, and the Humane Society of the United States (currently known as the Humane World for Animals). Her experience spans shelter operations, governance, capital campaigns, and nonprofit management. At every step, she has championed innovation, collaboration, and a people-centered approach to animal welfare.

At HSC, Moore led a successful multimillion-dollar capital campaign and the development of a new state-of-the-art Animal Resource Center. Her leadership has expanded services, deepened community partnerships, and positioned the organization as a vital resource for both pets and people in the Charlotte region. Her colleagues describe her as a rare blend of strength and empathy, transparency and wit. She creates a culture where people feel heard, celebrated, and empowered to lead.

Moore holds a Bachelor of Arts degree from the University of Maryland and is a graduate of the Johns Hopkins Nonprofit Management Program. She is a Certified Animal Welfare Administrator and has served on several national boards, including the Association for Animal Welfare Advancement and the National Federation of Humane Societies. She was also appointed to the National Companion Animal Advisory Committee by the Humane Society of the United States (currently known as the Humane World for Animals).

When she's not leading in the nonprofit world, Moore is likely planning her next travel adventure, getting happily lost in an art museum, or hunting down the best food and wine in a new city. A lifelong lover of culture and creativity, she finds joy in the unexpected moments that come with exploring the world. At home, she's kept on her toes by her three dogs—Sergio, Joey, and Rita—a lively crew with big personalities and zero respect for personal space. They keep her grounded and very entertained.

"It's not about taking credit. It's about planting a seed and watching it grow."

37

Carol Moulton

Plant the Seed: How Small Ideas Can Grow into Big Shifts in Animal Welfare

Every once in a while, we all get that lightbulb moment—a flash of inspiration for a new idea. But as soon as we start thinking about what it might take to bring that idea to life, it can quickly feel overwhelming. There's never enough time, never enough money, and always a long list of other projects already demanding our attention.

But I've learned over the years that if an idea has merit, there's usually a way to get it moving. And if it's a *really* good idea, others will often pitch in—or create their own version of it. Sometimes, leadership in animal welfare means simply sharing your idea with the world, so others can see its potential and build upon it, often far beyond your original dream.

For example, in the 1980s, I was Assistant Director at the Table Mountain Animal Shelter in Golden, Colorado. We handled animal control pickups from three different counties, as well as owner surrenders. Like many shelters at the time, we didn't have a veterinarian on staff. We relied on local practitioners who volunteered their time for emergencies—an animal hit by a car or suffering from an injury. But if an animal was sick, and not an emergency, we often had no choice but to euthanize. It was heartbreaking, but there were simply no other options.

A few years later, I joined the American Humane Association (AHA), which had been hosting national shelter conferences for decades. One day, that lightbulb went off. I thought, veterinarians who volunteer for shelters would probably love a chance to gather and share their experiences.

I wasn't sure I could make it happen, but I asked a representative from Gaines Pet Food for help funding speaker travel. He agreed, with one condition: that we include a session on pet nutrition. "*Deal*," I said.

At the same time, I had just met Dr. Patricia Olson, a professor at the University of Minnesota's vet school. She helped me connect with respected faculty from other schools, who agreed to speak on topics like disease control, intake procedures, shelter design, and animal health laws.

We advertised this new "shelter veterinarian" program alongside our regular AHA conference—at the same hotel, using the same promotional materials. That first year, only 30 people signed up. However, shelter veterinarians are some of the smartest and most dedicated professionals I've ever met, and they took the idea and ran with it.

Over the next few years, this program grew. National vet conferences, like the American Veterinary Medical Association and American Animal Hospital Association, began offering their own shelter medicine tracks. By 1999, Dr. Jan Scarlett and Dr. Lila Miller introduced the first-ever university course in shelter medicine at Cornell. In 2001, the University of California (UC) Davis launched the Koret Shelter Medicine Program—the world's first full clinical training and residency program in the field. Cornell was the first to bring it into the classroom; UC Davis was the first to establish a robust, clinical and research-based program. Together, they laid the foundation for what is now a recognized veterinary specialty.

I watched something similar happen with veterinary forensics. Dr. Olson authored one of the first guides for shelter veterinarians on recognizing signs of cruelty, just a 100-page booklet that AHA published. It was small, but it sparked something bigger. The ASPCA took that seed and expanded the work dramatically. Today, they publish extensive resources and offer externships to train veterinarians in this critical area.

So, what led us to believe this was necessary? Honestly, we saw the gaps. We didn't have the resources to launch national programs—we just started where we were, with what we had. And that was enough to get the ball rolling.

Of course, it's not about taking credit. It's about planting a seed and watching it grow. That's something I've come to believe deeply. If you put something valuable into the world, even something small, it can grow into something meaningful for animals, and for the people who serve them.

So, if I could offer one message to today's leaders, it would be this: Leadership isn't just about overseeing people. It's about seeing possibilities, identifying gaps, and helping others do more good than you could ever do alone. If you have an idea, don't wait. Put it out there. Build it. Share it. And if another organization picks it up and makes it even bigger or better, be glad—because that's leadership too.

Carol Moulton, M.A., *is a nationally respected leader in the animal welfare field with more than 40 years of experience in program development, communications, fundraising, and grant making. She began her career in 1976 as Publications Editor at The Humane Society of the United States (now known as Humane World for Animals) and went on to hold leadership roles at the American Humane Association where she developed groundbreaking initiatives in shelter medicine, early-age spay/neuter, and data-driven adoption strategies.*

During her tenure as Assistant Director for AHA's Animal Protection Division, Moulton was instrumental in launching the first continuing education programs for shelter veterinarians, helping establish the National Association of Shelter Veterinarians and shelter medicine as a recognized specialty. She also co-founded the National Council on Pet Population Study and Policy, leading research that redefined how shelters approach pet relinquishment and retention.

Moulton later served as the Manager of Charitable Giving for PetSmart Charities, where she managed over four million in annual grant giving, created new funding categories to support high-volume spay/neuter clinics, and participated in two national forums addressing critical adoption and population issues.

With a Master of Arts in Communication from the University of Denver, she has worked with dozens of national organizations throughout her career, including the ASPCA, Morris Animal Foundation, and The Delta Society, leaving a lasting impact on humane program strategy, grant writing, and fundraising across the animal welfare field.

"I've learned the importance of empowering others, trusting them to take ownership of their areas, and creating space for them to lead."

38

Jerrica Owen

Leading with Heart: 10 Leadership Lessons That Still Guide Me

Balancing day-to-day operations while staying focused on a long-term mission is one of the biggest challenges of leadership, especially in the animal welfare field, where both urgency and compassion are part of the daily rhythm. It's a balancing act I've learned to navigate over time and truthfully, through a fair share of trial and error. Here are 10 lessons that still guide me in this work.

1. Saying "Yes" Doesn't Always Serve the Mission

I have a naturally agreeable personality. I want to help, support, and say "yes" whenever I can because I care deeply about the work and the people doing it. But over the years, I've come to realize that trying to please everyone doesn't serve the mission. It can dilute our focus, exhaust our capacity, and sometimes create more harm than help.

2. Let the Mission Be Your Compass

One of the most important lessons I've learned is to lead with clarity. Every decision, whether it's responding to a daily challenge, evaluating a new opportunity, or setting strategic direction, gets filtered through the lens of our mission and long-term vision. I constantly ask myself: *Does this move us forward? Does it align with our core values?* That practice has become a compass, especially when things feel chaotic or overwhelming.

3. Empower Others So You Can Step Back

To keep things running smoothly on a day-to-day basis, I rely on a strong team, solid systems, and open lines of communication. I've learned the importance of empowering others, trusting them to take ownership of their areas, and creating space for them to lead. That approach enables me to step out of the weeds when needed, protecting time for strategic thinking, partnerships, and long-range planning without letting daily operations fall behind.

4. Pause Before Responding to What's Loudest

When competing priorities inevitably arise, I've had to learn to pause and evaluate. I ask: *Is this truly urgent, or just the loudest thing right now? Can someone else lead this effort? What's the cost of saying yes, and what might we unintentionally be saying no to?* That kind of honest assessment has helped me become a more intentional leader, even when the pressure is high.

5. Growth Often Comes Through Discomfort

I didn't get to where I am overnight. My leadership style has evolved significantly throughout my career, with a common thread being my willingness to continually work on myself. Emotional intelligence and self-reflection have become integral to my leadership approach. And while managing people never really gets easier, I've grown stronger, more self-aware, and more equipped to handle the tough parts. One thing I've learned is that growth often comes through discomfort. The moments I wanted to avoid, such as hard conversations, team tension, or realizing I didn't handle something the way I should have, have been my best teachers. When I can pause, reflect, and acknowledge my part, I emerge on the other side more prepared and grounded for the next challenge.

6. Stay Ambitious, Even When It's Hard

I think I've always had an ambitious streak—this drive to move forward and keep improving. I'm not entirely sure where it comes from, but it has been a consistent thread throughout my career. That ambition has helped me keep pushing, even when things were challenging or uncertain. Paired with emotional intelligence, it's helped me lead from a place of growth and adaptability.

Early in my career, I set my sights on earning my Certified Animal Welfare Administrator certification. At the time, I wasn't eligible, but that didn't stop me. I used it as motivation. With each promotion, I got one step closer. I kept saying "yes" to new challenges, stepping up whenever the opportunity came, and eventually, I got there. It wasn't quick, and it definitely wasn't easy, but staying focused on that long-term goal taught me a lot about perseverance and patience.

7. Leadership is Always a Work in Progress

If I could give my younger self advice, it would be: Believe in the long game. Be your own best advocate. And don't let setbacks shrink your goals. I would also remind myself that managing people is never going to be simple, but you get stronger the more you do it. You learn how to navigate personalities, build trust, hold people accountable with kindness, and lead through uncertainty. You learn to listen more, assume good intent, and communicate clearly even when it's hard.

8. Connection Beats Perfection

As I've grown, I've also developed a clearer understanding of the leadership qualities essential in animal welfare. At the top of that list? The ability to genuinely connect with people. So many of us are introverts by nature. We're drawn to animals for a reason! But the ability to sit down and have a real conversation with anyone, regardless of their title or background, is crucial.

Authenticity opens doors. It creates understanding. It builds bridges between departments, organizations, and communities.

9. Be Honest, Humble, and Human

Honesty and transparency are also non-negotiable. If I walk into a meeting and forget someone's name or can't recall the details I meant to bring, I own it. I don't pretend. I've learned that people respect a leader who's human. One who can admit when they don't have the answer or when something didn't go as planned. That kind of realness builds trust, and trust is the foundation of strong teams and lasting partnerships.

10. Presence Speaks Louder Than Position

Another trait I value deeply is presence. I've seen how powerful it is when a leader shows up, especially when they don't have to. Whether it's sitting in on a training, attending a community event, or supporting a team after a challenging field case, being there matters. It sends a clear message: I'm with you. And when your team knows you're present—not just in title, but in action—they're more likely to stay engaged and show up fully themselves.

In this field, leadership isn't about flash or ego. It's about humility, consistency, and care. Networking, being genuine, staying grounded...those things might not sound flashy, but they're everything. And they're especially important in a field like animal welfare, where compassion fatigue is real, where stakes are high, and where communities are counting on us to get it right.

Final Reflection: Keep Growing to Help Others Grow

There's no perfect formula for leadership. I've learned that again and again. But the leaders I admire most—and the kind I strive to be—are the ones who lead with intention and heart: who keep learning, keep showing up, and keep creating space for both people and animals to thrive.

To me, that's what leadership in this field is all about: showing up fully, staying human, and never stopping the work of growing—so you can help others grow too.

__Jerrica Owen__ is the Executive Director of the National Animal Care & Control Association, where she champions professionalism, progressive policies, and national standards for the animal services field. Owen joined NACA in 2021 as Director of Partnerships and Programs and was quickly promoted to Executive Director, a testament to her *passion, leadership, and extensive experience in the field. With a Bachelor of Science in Health Science from California State University, she has spent more than 20 years in animal welfare, serving in roles that span field operations, shelter management, emergency response, and strategic initiatives.*

Owen previously served as Director of Strategic Initiatives at San Diego Humane Society, where she helped lead organizational strategy, staff engagement, and emergency response. These included deployments during some of the country's most devastating disasters, where she supported both tactical and shelter operations for domestic animals, wildlife, and equines.

Owen is a Certified Animal Welfare Administrator and holds additional certifications in Lean Six Sigma Green Belt, Modern Human Resource Management, Organizational Leadership, and Mental Health First Aid. Her career has been defined by her ability to turn big-picture ideas into practical, real-world solutions that benefit animals, field officers, shelter teams, and the communities they serve. She is recognized for her dynamic leadership style, inclusive approach to industry engagement, and commitment to providing accessible resources for animal care and control professionals nationwide.

Based in California, Owen is a proud wife—and mother to human, furry, and shelled family members. She is also a certified USA Jump Rope Judge.

"We can build better systems if we choose to see the patterns, acknowledge the pain, and keep moving forward anyway."

Marc Peralta

From Music to Meaning—A Life Rewritten by Animals

I never set out to work in animal welfare, let alone become a leader in the field. My early career was spent in the music industry, where I promoted bands, managed venues, and lived in a world where long nights and loud shows were the norm. But after hitting a personal low point, including struggles with substance abuse, I knew I needed a complete reset. So, I sold my share of the business, went back to college, and on a whim, applied for a job at a local animal shelter.

It wasn't a calling; it was a practical choice. I didn't know how to do the work. But I needed a steady paycheck and something stable while I finished school. That job—meant to be a temporary gig—ultimately changed my life.

From Naivete to Awakening

I started as a kennel attendant. My first day was surprisingly fulfilling—cleaning kennels, preparing animals for adoption, and feeling a genuine sense of accomplishment. It was the first time in years I felt like I had done something that mattered. Then came day two.

Without warning or explanation, I was brought into *"the E. room"*—the euthanasia room. I was given controlled substances and asked to end the lives of animals I had just bonded with. There was no preparation, no debriefing, just a quiet expectation that I would go along with it. I didn't even know what questions to ask. That trauma still lives with me.

I quickly learned that euphemisms and routines often conceal deeper truths. Terms like *"red list"* and *"the room"* were ways to manage emotional discomfort. But I couldn't stop questioning. Why were we euthanizing animals when we had empty kennels? Why did time limits feel so arbitrary? The answers—*"this one is too old," "that one has been here two weeks," "we need space for possible hoarding cases"*—didn't sit right with me.

Learning to See the Patterns

That was my first pivotal leadership moment: realizing that not all mentorship is created equal. Just because someone had done something for decades didn't mean it was right. I needed to expand my sources of guidance and stop assuming tradition equaled truth.

Over time, I began to see the patterns. I noticed we repeated the same mistakes—over and over. In Los Angeles, I worked for Best Friends Animal Society as part of a community initiative called *No Kill Los Angeles*. When I first arrived, LA had a 56% save rate and a fractured network of stakeholders. From 1999 to 2009, Los Angeles Animal Services went through eight to ten general managers and assistant GMs. The cycle was so predictable it became part of the story: a new leader would be hailed, protested within a year, and gone soon after—sending the organization back to square one. The system couldn't stabilize because it lacked the necessary structure and collective trust to sustain leadership.

I knew we needed a different approach. I examined other movements, specifically the AIDS advocacy movement, and borrowed ideas on how to foster unity among people with diverse views. The goal wasn't to agree on everything; it was to commit to a shared outcome. By 2019, we had increased the save rate to 90%; not because we had eradicated conflict, but because we had created space for honest dialogue, grounded in shared goals and data, even when viewpoints differed.

One of the most important tools I used to reach people was to remind them of those patterns. The cycle of leadership turnover.

The resistance to data. The tendency to fight internally instead of directing energy toward progress. When you name the pattern, people start to see it, and once they see it, they are more open to different approaches.

From Efficiency to Empathy

My time in Los Angeles taught me how to bring people together and move a fractured system toward change. Earlier in my career, before LA, I was leading with a vastly different mindset.

In Philadelphia, I oversaw animal control and humane law enforcement for the entire state. We were responsible for tens of thousands of animals across multiple facilities. It was a high-pressure job, and I approached it with a sense of urgency. My leadership style was fast and results-driven. We improved live outcomes, but it came at a cost.

Turnover was high. Staff were burning out. I didn't realize how much damage that relentless pace could do, not just to my team, but to the culture I was creating.

Eventually, I learned that empathy isn't a soft skill; it's a survival skill. Slowing down helped me go farther. Leadership wasn't about being the smartest or fastest. It was about building cultures of shared goals and supporting people through change. I stopped making people the problem and started investing in systems that helped them thrive.

Pulling It All Together

What I learned in Philadelphia and Los Angeles forever reshaped how I showed up as a leader, but it also deepened my understanding of the emotional burden we all carry in this field. You can't lead in animal welfare without confronting the hard truth: we are a profession built on love but often surrounded by loss. And no matter how strategic or empathetic you become, you still have to reconcile what this work asks of you.

The lesson about empathy became even more important when I reflected on the emotional contradictions we carry in this work.

We love animals, and yet we euthanize them. We're told it's a kindness, even when our gut says otherwise. That's cognitive dissonance. And it's everywhere. I see it in staff who don't recognize how long stays deteriorate animals. I see it in decision-makers who say they support change but still cling to outdated policies.

As a leader, I've learned that the only way forward is to confront this dissonance with empathy, not judgment. People need space to wrestle with these contradictions, to be heard, and to be reminded that change is possible, even if it's hard. When people feel safe enough to face the pain—and to stop compartmentalizing the trauma they've been carrying—that's when transformation can begin.

Staying Motivated by Remembering Why

The trauma of euthanizing healthy animals still drives me. I work for Best Friends Animal Society not just because of its mission, but because I never want another young person to enter this field and be shattered by what they experience. There's enough trauma already. We can do better.

Leadership, to me, means helping shelter workers believe change is possible. It means reducing isolation, building efficiency, and protecting wellness for both animals and people. My motivation comes from remembering the person I was when I started in this field: naive, idealistic, and overwhelmed. I lead for that version of me—and for every kennel attendant still out there trying to make sense of a broken system.

This work comes at a cost. But the impact we can have on the world is immeasurable. We affect lives, both human and animal—every single day. If you're just starting out, don't wait to be perfect. You'll never master it all. None of us ever do.

Just start. Lead with your heart. And remember, we can build better systems if we choose to see the patterns, acknowledge the pain, and keep moving forward anyway.

Every small step matters—and it just might be the one that changes everything.

***Marc Peralta, MBA**, brings together many of Best Friends' programs and aligns all things related to the organization's direct lifesaving work as Chief Program Officer for Best Friends Animal Society. He also focuses on developing the knowledge and capabilities of individuals and more than 4,000 partner organizations nationwide, helping communities everywhere take practical, sustainable steps toward saving more lives.*

Peralta's path into animal welfare began nearly 20 years ago when he left work as an independent music promoter to become an Animal Care Attendant at the Humane Society of the Pikes Peak Region in Colorado Springs, Colorado. From those early hands-on days, he moved into leadership roles across the country, including Animal Care Manager at Nevada Humane Society, Vice President and Chief Operating Officer—and later interim CEO—at the Pennsylvania SPCA in Philadelphia, and served on the board of directors for the Animal Care and Control Team of Philadelphia.

Peralta joined Best Friends in 2012 as the executive director in Los Angeles, leading the city's lifesaving centers and the NKLA (No Kill Los Angeles) coalition for five years during a critical period in the city's shelter history. Today, his leadership spans Best Friends' network of programs, partnerships, and initiatives, ensuring teams have the tools, data, and collaborative support they need to make an impact.

Peralta holds an executive MBA from Brown University and IE University (Madrid, Spain), and a Bachelor of Arts degree in English from the University of Colorado. In 2017, Peralta co-founded Vintage Pet Rescue, a non-profit located in Rhode Island that is an adoption agency and sanctuary for senior, special needs, and geriatric pets.

"I always say, we're a basketball team, not a swim team. Everyone's on the same court. You pass, you defend, you support each other. We're not stuck in our lanes—we move together. That's how we win."

Brad Shear

Five Anchors That Shaped My Leadership

I didn't grow up dreaming of being a CEO—or even working in animal welfare. My path into leadership wasn't planned; it was shaped by watching my mother take on volunteer roles in our community, philosophy classes that taught critical thinking, and saying yes when someone needed help. Over the years, I have found myself in roles that required more than just managing people—they required steadiness, direction, and the ability to lead through both calm and crisis.

What I've learned is this: leadership doesn't come with a manual. It comes with a compass. And during the hardest moments of my career, from disaster response after Hurricane Katrina to rebuilding entire organizations, I've returned to a handful of steadying principles. These aren't strategies or buzzwords. They're anchors. They keep me grounded, clear, and focused—no matter what storm is rolling in.

Here are the anchors I come back to, again and again.

1. The Steady Anchor: Staying Calm in the Chaos

In the middle of a crisis, calm isn't just helpful—it's the anchor that steadies the entire ship.

One of the most defining moments of my career happened 20 years ago at the Lamar Dixon Expo Center in Louisiana—at the time, the largest animal evacuation site in U.S. history. It was established in response to Hurricane Katrina. There were four of us who flew in from Colorado, ready to lend a hand.

What we found were several enormous horse barns, each the size of a football field, filled with animals in crates, volunteers from across the country, and the kind of urgency you only see during a disaster. It was overwhelming for everyone. Local shelters had been destroyed. Many staff and rescuers had lost their homes, their belongings, and their sense of stability. Everyone was doing their best to help animals under unimaginable circumstances.

Of course, there wasn't a clear structure in place yet. But to us, coming from the outside, it was just an animal shelter without any walls. The animals still needed to be cleaned, fed, walked, and cared for.

My colleagues and I decided the best way we could help was to pick one area and bring some structure to it. I chose Barn 5 and got to work. I found a box of name tags, wrote *"Brad—Barn 5 Manager"* in Sharpie, stuck it on my chest, and walked in. I didn't have any official authority. I didn't ask for permission. I just said, *"Hi, I'm the new manager. Here's how we're going to do things."*

We built feeding and walking schedules. We assigned row leaders, ran medical checks, and grouped volunteers based on their skill sets. And 99% of the people there were relieved. They weren't waiting for a title; they were waiting for someone to step up and turn their panic into purpose.

That experience changed me. It was the first time I truly understood what leadership looks like in a crisis. It's not about control or authority—it's about structure and presence. When everything feels out of control, leadership is being the calmest person in the room.

2. The Listening Anchor: Holding Space Before Steering

Listening first keeps you grounded in perspective—and lets others feel the stability of their own voice.

I like to talk. But one of the best habits I've developed as a leader is to write down what I want to say and stay quiet until everyone at the table has spoken first.

Once the person in charge speaks, the dynamic in the room changes. People hesitate. They nod in agreement instead of thinking for themselves. So now, I bring a notepad to every meeting and write down what I want to say. I rarely say anything until everyone else has spoken. I want to hear what my team is thinking before they hear from me.

As a leader, it's easy for me to disagree with people. But I want to create a space where my team can disagree with me. That only happens if I hold back and let them speak first.

Leadership is about building a team that feels safe enough to challenge you, smart enough to solve problems together, and trusted enough to run without your constant input.

That's also why I make myself visible. I walk the shelter floor every day, say hello to staff and volunteers, and see for myself how the shelter feels. I park in the staff lot, even when someone suggested I get a reserved CEO spot. Because people watch everything you do. If you want people to believe you're a team, you must act like a teammate, not a title.

3. The Trusting Anchor: Releasing the Ropes to Let Others Lead

Authentic leadership isn't tightening control; it's trusting your crew and letting them steer.

One of the most significant shifts I've made as a leader is learning to relinquish control. That starts with being honest about what I don't know—and being completely okay with that. Early in my career, I felt pressure to have all the answers. Now, if a board member asks something I can't answer, I'll simply say, *"I don't know, but I'll find out."* That kind of honesty builds far more trust than pretending.

As I let go of needing to control everything, I began to realize the power of trusting others to lead. I've learned that trust isn't built through micromanagement. It's built by letting people shine. When someone on my team does something well, I make sure they get the credit. And when something goes wrong, I take the responsibility. That's the kind of leadership I respect—so that's the kind I try to model. Part of letting go is acknowledging that nobody is perfect. We can't let the perfect be the enemy of the good when delegating responsibility to others. If someone I've given responsibility to puts in the effort and gets things mostly right, I'm happy and can continue coaching for improvement.

Supporting growth is a key aspect of that trust. At the Potter League for Animals, we send staff to conferences, allocate time for webinars, and encourage them to share what they've learned with the team. Sometimes, we even encourage them to present their findings to the board. It's a way of saying: *your expertise matters, and we're all getting better together.*

But none of that works without a strong sense of teamwork. I always say, we're a basketball team, not a swim team. Everyone's on the same court. You pass, you defend, you support each other. We're not stuck in our lanes—we move together. That's how we win.

4. The Values Anchor: Keeping Decisions Moored in Purpose

When rules drift or don't apply, values are what hold you steady in ethical waters.

One of the most challenging aspects of animal welfare is striking a balance between the needs of an individual animal and those of the larger group or community. You want to save every animal. But sometimes you must step back and ask, "*What's the best decision for the whole system?*"—and that's uncomfortable. People want rules. They want certainty. But this work requires critical thinkers, not rule followers.

That's why I don't want to be the one answering every question. When someone's new, sure, I'll guide them. But the goal is to make it so they eventually don't need me; that they're making decisions based on values and experience, not instructions.

My degree is in philosophy, with a focus on values and social policy. It taught me how to think critically and how to help others do the same. One of the tools I use is the "Five Whys." You ask *"Why?"* five times to get to the root of an issue. The first answer is rarely the real one.

We often discuss this in our work: not every pit bull is the same. Not every case can be solved with a policy. And not every decision will make everyone happy. But if it's rooted in our values—compassion, transparency, and teamwork—it'll be the right one.

5. The Planning Anchor: Turning Drift into Direction

Ambition may launch the ship, but planning keeps it from drifting off course. Clear steps, honest timelines, and realistic expectations are the anchors that keep transformation afloat.

When I took my first CEO job at the Mohawk Hudson Humane Society in New York, I didn't know the right questions to ask. The building was falling apart. We were pulling half a million dollars a year from reserves, and we only had about three years left to survive.

But we turned it around. Over the next ten years, we grew from a $1.5 million to a $5 million budget. We rebuilt our reserves and opened a brand-new $7 million shelter, something no one thought was possible. But it wasn't magic. It was a vision, followed by lots of steps.

We had board members early on saying, *"Let's launch a capital campaign!"* And I had to say, *"We don't have the relationships to ask for six- or seven-figure gifts. Yet."*

So, we started small: launching direct mail, building our donor base, and investing in programs that rebuilt trust and credibility in our community. Slowly, we got there.

Change doesn't happen with ambition alone. It takes patience, restraint, and a real plan. That's true whether you're turning around a shelter or transforming a team.

Final Thoughts

If there's one thing I would tell a new leader, it's this: know what you're good at, see what you're not, and never be afraid to say, *"I don't know."*

Leadership isn't about control. It's about clarity. It's about giving people structure in chaos, space to speak, permission to think, and the support to lead alongside you.

People may not remember every policy you implemented, but they'll remember how they felt when you walked into the room. If they felt grounded, seen, and part of something bigger, then you were the anchor they needed.

***Brad Shear** has spent more than 30 years transforming animal welfare organizations into thriving, forward-thinking community resources, combining strategic vision with a hands-on commitment to improving the lives of both pets and people. As Chief Executive Officer of the Potter League for Animals in Middleton, Rhode Island, Shear has expanded the organization's programs, strengthened statewide partnerships, and acquired the state's largest spay and neuter clinic, ensuring more pets and people receive the care they deserve.*

Shear is a recognized leader in the field and a regular speaker at regional and national conferences. He has served as Board Chair for the Association for Animal Welfare Advancement, chaired its Best Practices and Emerging Trends Committee, and contributed to its Diversity, Equity, and Inclusion Committee. He also serves on the Hill's Pet Nutrition Shelter Advisory Council, the board of the New England Federation of Humane Societies, and the advisory committee for Supporting People and Animal Relationships for Change (SPARC).

Throughout his career, from managing shelters in New York City and Boulder to founding the New York State Animal Protection Federation, Shear has focused on building strong, sustainable systems that improve outcomes for animals and the people who care for them. His work has earned numerous accolades, including the Badge of Honor from the Albany County District Attorney's Office, the President's Medal from Excelsior College, the Community Hero Award from Unity House of Troy, and the Changemaker Organization of the Year Award from CARE, a global humanitarian organization, in 2023.

Originally from New York City, Shear holds a degree from the University of Colorado at Boulder and now lives in Peace Dale, Rhode Island, with his wife, two children, one dog, and two cats. He continues to lend his expertise to national and regional boards, mentoring the next generation of animal welfare leaders.

"You are not above your team—you are in service to them."

Katherine McGowan Shenar

What I Wish I Knew: Five Lessons from 30 Years in Animal Welfare Leadership

After three decades in the animal welfare field, I've learned more than I ever could have imagined—some lessons arrived gently, others arrived like lightning bolts. However, the most transformative lessons came when I had to stretch beyond what I thought I knew, challenge my beliefs, and grow into a leader who truly serves others. Here are the five most important lessons I wish I had known as a first-time leader.

1. Passion is powerful, but it must evolve with knowledge.

You will enter this field with deeply held values. They may be rooted in your childhood, shaped by early experiences, or inspired by people you admire. These values give you purpose, but they can also become blinders.

When I started in 1996, I absorbed everything I could. One myth I took to heart was that black cats were at risk of ritual sacrifice during Halloween. For seven years, I led a well-intentioned but deeply misguided campaign to protect black cats: removing them from the adoption floor, issuing public warnings, and promoting media stories about the supposed dangers to them.

I was passionate. I believed I was saving lives. But the reality? Many of those cats, removed from view, became stressed, ill, and were euthanized. The myth I believed had no data to support it, and the harm it caused was very real.

That experience humbled me. I learned to ask better questions, seek evidence, consult experts, and remain open to the possibility of being wrong. Passion without inquiry can lead us astray. Let your values inspire you, but let science and experience guide your actions.

2. The frontline holds the answers. Listen to them.

As leaders, we spend our days in meetings, planning strategy, fundraising, and collaborating with external stakeholders. However, the heartbeat of our mission is happening at the front desk, in adoption counseling rooms, and on the phone with pet owners as they make tough decisions. When we distance ourselves from these moments, we lose touch with how our mission unfolds day by day.

Over the years, I've seen well-meaning leaders make decisions in a vacuum, unaware that a small change could create a huge ripple effect. Technology evolves. Community needs shift. Protocols improve. The people who know this best? The staff who live it daily.

The best decisions I've made have come from listening to those closest to the work. Ask questions. Shadow their work. Create space for honest feedback. Leadership isn't about having the answers. It's about seeking them from the people who do.

3. We all carry bias — and that matters.

Leadership requires self-awareness. We each bring our own lived experiences, upbringings, educations, and identities into every conversation. That shapes how we see the world, and how we judge others.

Years ago, I prided myself on stepping in to help at the front desk. I thought I was being supportive. But I made mistakes. I misunderstood protocols. I admitted animals into the program that didn't meet criteria. I created more stress for the staff, not less.

And in quieter ways, my own worldview shaped how I judged pet owners. As a white, middle-class woman, I held an unconscious bias about what a "good" pet home looked like. That bias led me to make assumptions that weren't fair, and animals likely missed out on loving homes as a result.

The lesson? Acknowledge your lens. Seek out perspectives that challenge it. Leadership is not about always being right. It's about being open, accountable, and committed to doing better.

4. Onboarding isn't a checklist. It's a foundation.

When a new staff member joins your team, you have one chance to set the tone for their success. That first year is your greatest opportunity to shape their mindset, teach critical skills, and immerse them in your culture.

Too often, overwhelmed organizations rush onboarding. We throw new employees into the deep end and hope they swim. And then we're surprised when they leave within six months.

Onboarding should be structured, intentional, and sustained. It should introduce not just job tasks, but the "why" behind your work. It should offer training, mentorship, and regular feedback. It's not a luxury; it's a leadership responsibility.

5. Your team's success is your success.

One of the hardest and most important lessons: your success as a leader is entirely dependent on the people you lead. You are not above them—you are in service to them.

Great leaders understand that their job is to lift burdens, remove roadblocks, and ensure their team has the tools and support they need to thrive. You are the coach, not the star player. When things go wrong, look inward first. Ask: *What didn't I provide? What clarity was missing? How can I be more helpful?*

Then, ask your team—regularly and sincerely—the following questions:

"What do you need from me?"

"How can I support you better?"

"What's getting in your way?"

Leadership is not about control; it's about empowerment. When you set clear expectations, provide training, and create space for feedback, you build a team that can excel. And, when they do, so will you.

These five lessons continue to guide me, and I offer them to you with the hope that they'll serve you on your own journey. Leadership in animal welfare is complex, emotional, and deeply rewarding. And the more we commit to growing ourselves, the more good we can do—for animals, for communities, and for the teams who make our mission possible.

***Katherine McGowan Shenar, M.A.**, is a transformative leader in animal welfare, currently serving as Executive Vice President of The Association for Animal Welfare Advancement. With more than three decades of experience, she champions innovation, collaboration, and professional development for animal welfare leaders nationwide. Her expertise spans executive leadership, organizational culture, coalition building, marketing communications, and fundraising, making her a catalyst for progress across the profession.*

As the host of The Intake Podcast, Shenar facilitates thoughtful conversations on emerging trends and the real-world challenges animal welfare professionals face. Her career began in media and advertising before she found her calling in 1996 as Director of Public Relations and Marketing at the Humane Society of Missouri in St. Louis, Missouri. Since then, she has held leadership roles with the Animal Protective Association of Missouri, the Humane Society of the United States (currently known as Humane World for Animals), Asheville Humane Society, and San Diego Humane Society.

Shenar is also the author of "Coalition Building for Animal Care Organizations," a practical guide to uniting animal advocates through collaboration. She holds a Master of Arts in Media Communications and currently lives in Washington state with her husband, four dogs, and a cat. She remains deeply committed to advancing the field and welcomes connections on LinkedIn.

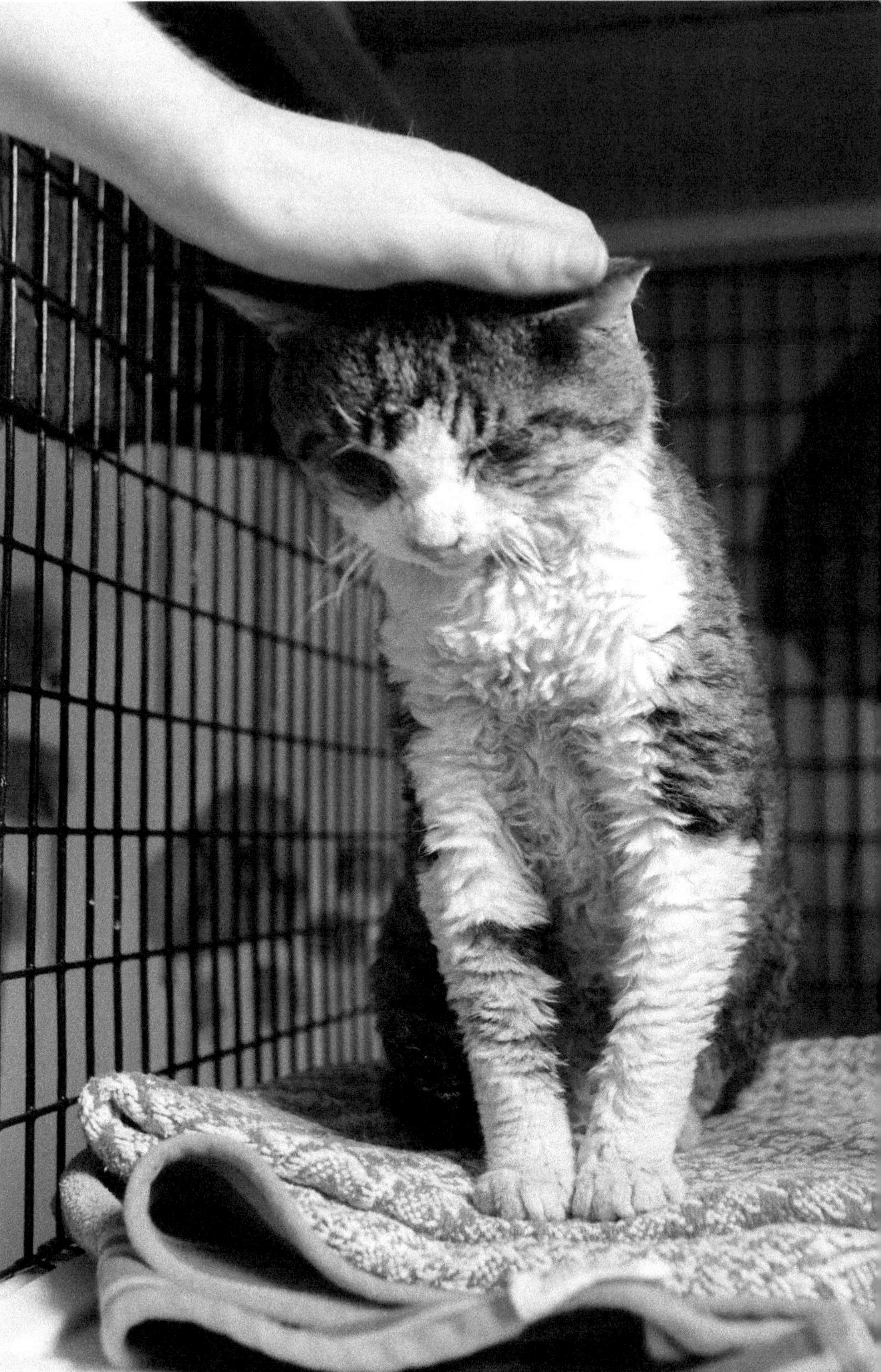

"If you're just getting started (in this field), it can be overwhelming. It is unpredictable, challenging and absolutely worth it."

Jess Townsend

Stepping Away from Sheltering Led to My Greatest Challenge

I told the universe I wanted to run my own shelter.

Apparently, I was not specific enough about that request. The shelter gods have a sense of humor and love to mess with us, and they overdelivered on this request in a big way. (Hang around any shelter long enough and you'll know exactly what I mean!)

In my 13th year of sheltering, and 41st year of life, I took a break. I had been the Director of Operations at a shelter for almost six years when the COVID-19 pandemic hit. Figuring out the first six months of the pandemic sucked the joy out of me. I didn't look forward to going to my empty, silent shelter, devoid of happy adopters, kids working on humane education projects, and volunteers walking dogs or petting cats. I wasn't sure anymore if sheltering was what I wanted to do, or just what I did.

I spoke with my husband and family, and we made some adjustments. We sold our house, moved in with my recently widowed father, and I enrolled in graduate school full-time, taking a year away from my work in animal welfare.

A Return to Chaos (and Dogs)

The master's degree program I chose was in Policy, Planning, and Management. I already had over a decade of on-the-job training in shelters, but I wanted academic leadership education to complement it. I finished 90% of the program in a year. Around the time I was getting itchy to rejoin the world, a friend at a nearby shelter reached out to ask a question they knew I would know the answer to. They also happened to mention they were looking for a Director of Operations.

As it turned out, I still loved sheltering. I had become the crazy lady on the sidewalk begging to pet your dog with overwhelming enthusiasm. I missed the animals, the people, and the mostly controlled chaos that makes our days go by so quickly.

Thinking I could easily finish the rest of my courses while doing a job I knew well, I dove in. Within six weeks, I was the interim Executive Director, responsible for two shelter locations with decades of deferred maintenance, a thrift store, and a distressed building project. I was not specific enough when I said I wanted to run a shelter. I should have made many more stipulations before I put it out into the universe, but by then, it was too late. I was all in.

The Apology Tour and the Armageddon File

That first year was the most challenging of my life. The building project lacked a capital campaign to cover even half of its costs, and the construction contract would deplete the organization's reserves. It was too late to stop it; the property had been purchased, a mortgage taken out, the contracts signed, and construction begun.

The board of directors was down to only three people, the director of development stopped coming to work, and the director of finance, Ruth, started the same week I did.

I launched what I called "The Apology Tour." If musicians can name their tours, so can I. I spoke with anyone who would speak with me—community members, businesses, and donors. Many had walked away due to a lack of stewardship and visibility from the organization. Meanwhile, I was holding down three roles—executive director, director of operations, and director of development. I split my time between rectifying shelter operations issues, raising money, and managing the building project, all while attempting to reset public perception.

We exited staff who weren't aligned with the level of customer service and animal care we needed. Ruth dove deep into the financial rabbit hole and I worked six to seven days a week. Some days, I was on the floor doing animal care or customer service all day, then made dinner at home and spent the rest of the night on the couch doing my "actual" jobs.

Reward Systems and Burnout Warnings

It was exhausting but also exhilarating. My personal reward system for work is a sense of responsibility. This reward system can be a trap in an animal shelter if you are not careful. The shelter can be a black hole of need, and you can pour yourself into it so much that you have nothing left for yourself, your family, and your friends. I came very close to doing just that during this time.

However, we completed the new building and relocated the shelter by the following June. It was touch-and-go for a while; would we finish the building and meet the obligations of the construction contract just to have to close our doors? Ruth kept the "Armageddon File" for me, which outlined cash projections for when we would run out of money and how downsizing staff would impact operational revenue. I could ask her on any given day what the prediction was for D-Day, the day we could no longer pay our bills, and she could tell me.

I haven't asked for a D-Day report in almost a year.

Rebuilding the Right Way

We're not out of the woods, but we're in far better shape than we were three years ago. We now have a Director of Operations and a Director of Development. Even if I were inclined to continue the frenetic schedule I started with (and I'm not), no one can juggle that many roles and do them well. We've carefully added staff, listened to the team, and found creative ways to assign responsibilities.

It's fun bouncing ideas off the team and not having someone to tell me, *"No, you can't do that."* It's also terrifying. Because when things go wrong, they land squarely on my shoulders.

I haven't done a caregiving shift in over a year, but I still can. I can clean kennels or cat habitats, counsel adopters, vaccinate, draw blood, euthanize, conduct intake evaluations, and handle difficult patrons. I can manage the building systems when they go haywire or help juggle space when we seem to have more pets than spaces for them. And that matters. Being able to do the jobs others do builds credibility and camaraderie. It changes how your team sees you and how they speak with you. It gives you the perspective that leaders without frontline experience simply don't have. Everyone has a first job in animal welfare, but real leadership requires knowing how all the parts of the shelter fit together. And that understanding only really comes from doing the work.

Shelter Life Forever

I still find my role both exhilarating and exhausting. There are far easier ways to make a living—even in the nonprofit world. But I would argue that there are few rewards more meaningful than being part of a successful, well-run animal shelter.

And, because once again I wasn't clear enough with the universe, and because the shelter god's love to mess with us, our second facility now needs replacing. Oh, and the thrift store storage house? There's a stream running through the basement, and a tree just hit the roof in the last windstorm.

It's always something. And it probably always will be.

If you're in this work, you already know what I mean. If you're just getting started in animal welfare, brace yourself. It's messy and unpredictable, but absolutely worth it.

And if the shelter gods come for you, too, just know, you're not alone. Welcome to the club and to the joy of saving lives.

***Jess Townsend, MPPM,** got her passion for animal welfare by volunteering with a cat rescue group, setting her on a path that would become her life's work. With a master's degree in policy, planning, and management from the University of Southern Maine, a degree in psychology and studio art from Providence College, and a background in graphic design and marketing, Jess brought a unique blend* *of skills that prepared her to turn that passion into a career serving pets in need and the people who love them.*

Townsend began her journey in 2007 at the Maryland SPCA in Baltimore, Maryland, where she took her first professional steps into sheltering. In 2009, she joined the Washington Humane Society (now the Humane Rescue Alliance) in Washington, D.C., where she spent five years helping drive lifesaving innovation. It was here that she learned to manage staff and programs in a large urban shelter, balancing the complexities of people, pets, and resources.

Returning to New England, Townsend spent six years as Director of Operations at the Animal Refuge League of Greater Portland in Westbrook, Maine. There she oversaw daily operations, guided the team through growth and change, and built systems that improved outcomes for both animals and people.

In 2021, Townsend became the Executive Director of Midcoast Humane in Brunswick, Maine, stepping into the role during a time of extraordinary challenges. She led the organization through a major building project, a staffing crisis, and a full-scale operational restructuring. Known for her hands-on leadership and strategic thinking, Townsend is deeply committed to building strong teams and creating shelter systems that are resilient and enduring.

Outside of the shelter, Townsend has two step kids, four cats, two dogs, and a husband and says, only partly kidding, that nothing else that needs to be fed or see any kind of doctor gets to live in her home. So, she took up gardening to help manage stress. She is now responsible for maintaining multiple gardens in her free time and is hatching plans to rewild the rest of her yard as a pollinator habitat.

"Leadership doesn't always arrive with a title. Sometimes, it walks in quietly, ready to listen, ready to learn."

Misty Valenta

No Role Too Small: How Volunteering Shaped My Leadership

During my rounds through the kennel one day, I noticed a dog had tipped over his water bowl. I stepped in, righted the bowl, and started filling it from the hose. That's when a longtime volunteer rounded the corner, paused, and asked, *"What are you doing?"*

I told him I was just giving the dog a refill, and he said, *"Yeah, but directors don't do that."*

That moment has stuck with me ever since. My response was probably something like, *"Well, I do."* It felt like a line in the sand—one that defines who I am as a leader. No position is too big to fill a water bowl. No title exempts you from compassion. That's the kind of director I always wanted to be.

How a Volunteer Shift Became a Career

I grew up in San Antonio, Texas, in a neighborhood where dogs didn't come from shelters. They came from neighbors, from street corners, from the sound of puppies crying under a porch. We knew which dogs belonged to which houses because the dogs roamed freely. They were savvy, aware of traffic, people, and the rhythms of the community. One even dug a hole near my grandmother's house and had her puppies there—on Christmas Eve.

That's how I got Olive, my first dog as an adult. She was a little Christmas Eve pup named after *Olive, the Other Reindeer*, and I had no idea what I was doing. I was teaching elementary school at the time, thriving in the organized chaos of the classroom but drowning in the bureaucracy outside of it. I signed up for a basic manners class for Olive at the local humane society to give her and I time to work together.

My background in education, theater, and storytelling aligned perfectly with what I was learning about positive reinforcement in dog training. Olive thrived. I did, too. I was geeking out over learning theory with dogs, as it was similar to what I studied in college. One of the trainers pulled me aside one day and said, *"You should volunteer at the shelter."*

So, I did. I started volunteering on weekends and in the evenings to walk dogs and teach them basic manners. It suddenly became the thing I looked forward to most. The people I met were passionate and kind. The work filled my cup in a way that teaching no longer did. I was just hitting my five-year mark—a common burnout milestone for teachers—when I saw a posting for an adoption counselor at the shelter. I quit my teaching job and told myself I would work in this position for a year. Just to see if I liked it.

Within months, I moved into a community programs coordinator role. I wasn't chasing promotions. I was following my passion, and the path kept unfolding before me. Then came the Bastrop, Texas, wildfires followed closely by a hoarding case involving over 100 dogs. I was dropped into real crises. And to my surprise, I thrived. The chaos didn't rattle me. I could think clearly, stay calm, and organize when others were spinning. That's when I realized: I wanted to do more than respond to emergencies. I wanted to be on the front lines every day, where I could meet people in the middle of their own personal emergencies and offer real-time solutions.

That decision led me to the Williamson County Regional Animal Shelter in Georgetown, Texas—a regional shelter with an open door. And let me tell you, the front lines look different. You never know who's coming through that door, what they're going through, or how you can help. Some days, it's a family rehoming a beloved pet because of eviction. Other days, it's someone bringing in a litter of puppies they didn't plan for. Either way, you must be prepared—not just with answers, but with empathy. I wanted to be proactive and deeply rooted in the community. I felt I could only do that by working for an open-intake shelter.

At an open-intake shelter, you don't have the luxury of waiting for someone else to solve the problem. You're in it every day—with real people, real situations, and real urgency. I began to see that success in this work wasn't just about policy or process. It was about people—*all* the people, including staff, volunteers, and the community. And I realized something else, too: the best ideas and strongest outcomes occur when you engage the community—because the more hands involved, the better.

Many Hands, One Mission

It's been 15 years since I took that first job as an adoption counselor, and one truth has only grown clearer with time: we can't do this work alone. Saving lives takes more than passion—it takes people. People who clean kennels and greet adopters. People who walk dogs, comfort trembling cats, answer phones, and open their hearts just a little wider every time it's needed. It takes staff, volunteers, and the community working side by side. Every hand matters. Every role matters. None of us can do this alone.

But let's be honest; volunteer-staff relationships in shelters haven't always been easy. There are often different expectations and different understandings of the work we do. Sometimes, even tension. At our shelter, we've worked hard to change that.

One of the simplest changes we made was renaming our shirts. Instead of "Staff" and "Volunteer," we now wear shirts that say "Lifesaver" and "Volunteer Lifesaver." It's a small shift, but a powerful one. It reminds us—and the public—that we are all here for the same reason. We are all lifesavers. We are all part of this mission.

That spirit of shared purpose is something I fight to protect every day. I want everyone—staff and volunteers—to feel valued and empowered. One of the ways I try to model that is by starting team meetings with, *"I have a crazy idea. What if..."* And now, others do the same. They pitch ideas. They speak up. They dream forward. Because they know their voice matters.

Fostering that kind of culture requires more than structure—it requires trust, and the willingness to grow. There's a quote I come back to often: *"Do the best you can until you know better. Then when you know better, do better."* That's Maya Angelou. And it applies to shelters just as much as it does to people.

When You Know Better, You Lead Better

There was a time when shelters did the best they could with what they had. And for many of us, that was enough because it had to be. But today, we know better. We know that treating the community like the enemy gets us nowhere. Saving lives isn't about blame; it's about collaboration. Real change doesn't come from working harder in isolation. It comes from working together, smarter, with humility and heart.

That's the kind of culture I want to lead. One where every person and every idea is welcomed. One where the mission is shared. One where the next great leader might be the person quietly filling a water bowl.

Because that was me. Volunteering changed my life. It taught me that leadership isn't about standing apart, it's about leaning in. And now, as a director, I try to leave the door open behind me for the next person who wanders in, not quite sure what they're doing, but ready to fill that water bowl and begin their journey.

__Misty Valenta__ is the Director of Animal Services at the Williamson County Regional Animal Shelter (WCRAS), a nationally recognized open-admission shelter in Georgetown, Texas. Since stepping into the role in 2020, she has helped transform WCRAS into a collaborative, lifesaving model, prioritizing transparency, innovation, and a culture where both people and animals thrive. Valenta previously served for eight years as the Community Programs Coordinator, where she expanded the shelter's foster, volunteer, and rescue partnerships while building out its fundraising, marketing, and outreach efforts.

With a background in development and communications at the Austin Humane Society in Austin, Texas, and early experience as an educator and events coordinator, Valenta brings a rare blend of creativity and operational savvy to her work. She has built bridges across departments and communities to increase engagement and improve outcomes for both animals and people.

In 2023, Valenta joined the Best Friends Animal Society's National Strategic Council, helping shape the future of animal sheltering nationwide. She also serves as a board member for Fans of WCRAS and remains deeply connected to the community she serves. Valenta believes that true shelter leadership isn't about standing apart; it's about lifting others, creating space for ideas to grow, and recognizing that the next great leader might already be among us.

Ledy VanKavage

Fighting for Change to Save Lives

Like many of you, I have always loved dogs. Growing up, my pit bull, Boody, was my best friend. My Lithuanian grandmother had found him as a stray pup, and I was smitten. He went everywhere with me, and my mom knew I was safe if Boody was with me.

I've always loved animals but never envisioned that I would become an animal advocate. In 1984, I had just graduated from law school. There was no such thing as "animal law." I had never attended a county board or city council meeting. That year I discovered that my county—the county I had lived in my entire life—was selling animals for research. I was outraged and decided to act. I formed the Madison County Coalition to Stop Pound Seizure with my husband, Cliff Froehlich, and three animal lovers/activists: Jeff Miller, Christie Walker, and Dorothy English.

Grassroots Beginnings

We did not go off on this initiative half-cocked. We researched and attended county board meetings to identify the key players on the board. We started petitions and gathered signatures to change the inhumane policy. We knocked on doors, made calls to county board members, and encouraged pet lovers to make calls. We were able to secure a prominent county board member as a sponsor for the resolution to halt the pound seizure. The coalition then presented our petitions, which had almost 1,000 signatures, to the county clerk.

We asked to see the statistics for the shelter. We were devastated. In 1984, over 4,000 dogs and cats came into the county facility, but only 78 dogs and 14 cats were adopted out. The rest were either sent for experimentation or euthanized in a gas chamber.

I went to the County Board members and said, *"Let us form a humane society and handle your adoptions."* They agreed, and that is how we founded the Madison County Humane Society, now known as the Metro East Humane Society in Madison County, Illinois. We started with nothing but the determination to make change and save lives. We had to rent three dog pens and nine cat cages from the Madison County Pound—one pen for male dogs, one for female dogs, and one for puppies. The conditions were bleak.

Taking on the System

At the time, our relationship with animal control was unfortunately adversarial, but we were determined. The officers were union members who viewed us as a threat and a nuisance, and they were resistant to change. They liked the status quo. We just wanted to save lives, but it was difficult given the strained relationship. But we persevered and were extremely fortunate when PetSmart opened a store in a neighboring town and they wanted us to bring dogs and cats to the store for adoption. Our adoption events were extremely successful, and in the first year, we adopted around 800 dogs and cats. The following year, we adopted over 1,000 dogs and cats, mostly at PetSmart. The Madison County Humane Society even received an award at the PetSmart Charities annual meeting that year for outstanding adoption performance.

Eventually, we realized that being located in the animal control building was untenable and that we needed to raise funds for our own building. We convinced the county to deed us an acre of land adjacent to the Madison County Pound, allowing us to easily run their adoption program. But we failed to realize that we were challenging another powerful status quo at the time—the veterinary community.

Zoning Battles and Community Support

Despite the acre being next door to the pound, we needed to get a zoning variance to build the shelter. That's when a local veterinarian, with the help of some of the animal control officers, decided to oppose the rezoning. It was a battle that required our members to mobilize and knock on every door in the township. Almost 100 supporters attended the subsequent zoning hearing, but so did the veterinarian and some of the neighbors opposing the rezoning for the building. Unfortunately, after the hearing, the Zoning Board of Appeals denied our permit.

But we didn't give up. We petitioned the County Board to override the decision of the Zoning Board of Appeals. The County Board rarely overruled the Zoning Board, but after all our members lobbied them, they did in this instance—and we were able to build a home of our own.

Changing the Culture

Over the years, canny politicians realized the benefits of declaring a community goal of operating a no-kill shelter. The incoming administration hired a new director, Katherine Conder, an animal lover who was committed to lifesaving. Katherine was a former special education teacher who knew nothing about animal control but wanted to try new things. She made a huge difference in changing the culture at the pound, although some of the old animal control wardens were either let go or chose to retire.

Currently, Metro East Humane Society has a collaborative working relationship with animal control. The Metro East Humane Society and Best Friends Animal Society helped the county enact a community cat ordinance, and the trap-neuter-vaccinate-return program is saving many lives. Their cat save rate is 89% -- almost at the no-kill benchmark of 90%. They have even started having playgroups through *Dogs Playing for Life* and are doing adoptions and fostering. They have evolved with the times and are no longer the Madison County Pound. They are the Madison County Animal Care and Control, and they are on their way to becoming a no-kill organization.

As for Metro East Humane Society, they are able to employ two veterinarians, and many veterinarians in the community help with special medical cases. Like animal control, many veterinarians now recognize the value in collaborating with humane societies and increasing the adoption of dogs and cats.

The Power of Persistence

This arduous, but worthwhile journey has taught me that a small group of determined people can change everything.

As Margaret Mead said, *"Never doubt that a small group of thoughtful committed individuals can change the world. In fact, it's the only thing that ever has."*

Politics is not a spectator sport. It is up to you to get active and organize.

Success in animal welfare rarely comes from one person acting alone. It's the result of many people pooling their strengths, perspectives, and resources under strong, shared leadership. Collaboration allows us to tackle challenges from every angle, whether it's navigating local politics, overcoming entrenched practices, or dismantling outdated policies. When you face resistance—whether from decision-makers, systemic roadblocks, or even just plain hostility—lean on your team, conduct thorough research, stay organized, and keep pushing forward together.

Ultimately, leadership rooted in persistence and collaboration will foster safer, more humane communities for both people and animals. And when you look back, you'll see that every conversation, every compromise, and every shared victory made the effort worthwhile.

***Ledy VanKavage, Esq.**, is the Senior Legislative Attorney for Best Friends Animal Society, where she works to advance humane policies nationwide. A passionate advocate for animals since the 1980s, Ledy first entered the field after discovering her county was selling shelter pets for research—a revelation that led her to co-found the Madison*

County Coalition to Stop Pound Seizure and later the Metro East Humane Society. Her grassroots beginnings shaped a career devoted to saving lives through collaboration, legal reform, and persistence.

Before joining Best Friends, VanKavage served as Senior Director of Legislation and Legal Training for the ASPCA, helping to spearhead the passage of more than 50 humane state laws during her tenure. She is a past chair of the American Bar Association's Animal Law Committee and has co-authored the U.S. Department of Justice publication, "The Problem of Dog-Related Incidents and Encounters." She also serves as an instructor for the Illinois Law Enforcement Training and Standards Board.

VanKavage's work has been recognized with numerous honors, including the American Bar Association's Excellence in Animal Law Award, the Wallace Award from the Wallace the Pit Bull Foundation, and the Women in Government Relations' Excellence in a State Campaign Award. She has been featured on MSNBC (currently known as MS NOW) and NPR, and in Time, the Chicago Tribune, and The New York Times.

From grassroots activism to national policy, VanKavage's career is defined by her unwavering belief that a small, determined group of people can change the world for animals—and that true leadership is measured not only by victories won, but by the persistence to keep fighting until they are.

"Animal welfare is not about animals instead of people. It's about both. The human-animal bond is sacred. And the stronger that bond is in our communities, the stronger we all become."

Mike Wheeler

A Journey into Humane Leadership: From Kennels to Community

I didn't grow up dreaming of working in animal welfare. On our family farm, animals played a role—providing food, offering protection, and serving as a means of hunting—but they weren't "pets" in the way I now understand the term. I wasn't an animal lover in the traditional sense. I didn't grow up seeing animals as companions, but as tools for living.

After serving in the Army, I moved to Colorado and built a thriving insurance business. On paper, things looked perfect. But in 2008, my wife and I made a life-altering decision. We left the success and financial comfort of our business behind to move home to Arkansas, all for one reason: a better future for our four children. No amount of money could compete with their education and upbringing. It was one of the first big decisions that made me realize how leadership often starts not in boardrooms—but in sacrifice.

From Business Success to Kennel Duty

When it was time to return to work, I didn't want to re-enter the corporate world. I wanted to do something meaningful. That's how I found myself accepting a job with the city as an Animal Control Officer—making $9 an hour cleaning kennels and issuing citations.

A few years in, our Animal Services Director misappropriated a donation. I had a choice: stay silent or speak up. I chose the hard right over the easy wrong. He was removed, and I was offered the chance to step into the role. I wasn't prepared, but I knew I cared. So I stepped forward—headfirst into leadership—with more questions than answers.

Early on, I led by the book. Literally, every ordinance, every law—I enforced them with rigid clarity. If you broke the rules, there were consequences. Period. That black-and-white mindset made sense to me at the time. But I was missing something big: The people. Their stories. Their struggles. Their humanity.

That realization hit me the hardest after a particularly difficult call. An elderly woman, 93 years old, had overfed her dog to the point of neglect. I confiscated the pet, doing what I thought was right by the law. Within months, the woman passed away, and so did her dog. I still believe it was heartbreak and loneliness that took them both. That moment cracked something in me. I began to question the way we approached enforcement. Were we always doing what was *right*, or just what was *written*?

Other calls taught me painful lessons, like the time I picked up a couple of loose dogs and issued citations instead of simply placing them back in their fenced yard. The family couldn't afford the reclaim fees. That led to arrest warrants, a suspended driver's license, job loss—a cascade of consequences far more damaging than a hole in a fence. I began to see how our systems, though well-intentioned, could unintentionally harm the very people we were supposed to help.

"No" isn't an Answer: It's a Challenge.

In 2017, I visited Austin Pets Alive as part of a Maddie's Fund apprenticeship. What I witnessed there changed me again. In less-than-ideal conditions, they were saving lives at a scale I hadn't thought possible. Dr. Ellen Jefferson, in particular, inspired me. She taught me to question everything: policies, practices, assumptions. She showed me that passion wasn't enough—we needed data, strategy, and relentless belief in possibility. From her, I learned that "no" isn't an answer: It's a challenge.

From that point on, my leadership began to evolve. I transitioned from enforcer to educator, from rule follower to relationship builder. I began making decisions that prioritized the human-animal bond, not just the statutes on a page. Our department started changing with me. We moved from punishment to prevention, from citations to conversations.

The most rewarding part of this work has never been the awards or recognition—it's been watching our city become more compassionate, one person and one pet at a time. I see it in kids walking dogs adopted from our shelter. I hear it in stories of neighbors helping return a lost pet home—without ever calling animal control. I feel it when I attend vaccine clinics and see families taking pride in keeping their pets healthy. That's success, and no chart can capture it.

I've also learned that leadership means letting go. It means trusting your team and making space for them to lead. I used to think I had to control everything. Now, I manage my calendar so I can be out in the community while my small, but mighty team handles day-to-day operations—with my guidance, not my micromanagement.

Burnout is real in this field. I haven't figured out how to eliminate it, but I've learned to fight it by focusing on the good. Yes, we face tragedy. Yes, we lose animals. But every day we also reunite pets with their families. We educate. We prevent suffering. That's the fuel that keeps me jumping out of bed, smiling, ready to go.

Growing Leaders, Not Just Managing Staff

Over time, hiring has become one of my most strategic responsibilities. We don't just hire "animal people." We hire "people-people." We can teach how to clean kennels, give vaccines, or handle a catch pole. What we can't teach is empathy.

When I hire someone, I tell them this: *"I hope one day you take my job."* We train every employee to understand every part of the organization. And when other agencies need leadership, I encourage my people to apply. That's how we grow the field—by building leaders, not just staff.

I still don't think of myself as a leader. It feels strange to offer leadership advice. But if I had to, I would say this: Care deeply. Care about your team. Care about your community. Care enough to do what's right, even when it's hard. And thank the people who make it all possible—because we can't return a single lost dog without an owner to claim it, or adopt one out without someone willing to open their home.

Animal welfare is not about animals *instead* of people. It's about both. The human-animal bond is sacred. And the stronger that bond is in our communities, the stronger we all become.

I didn't set out to become a leader in animal welfare. I just kept showing up. I made mistakes. I learned. I kept choosing the hard path—the one paved in empathy, trust, and shared humanity. And somewhere along the way, I realized this work isn't just about saving animals. It's about building a more compassionate world—for *everyone*.

***Mike Wheeler** has been the Director of Community Services for Cabot Animal Support Services, Arkansas, since 2009, armed with a singular mission: advancing animal welfare and public safety through compassion-driven innovation. Under his leadership, the city's open-admission animal shelter and animal control operations have become a model for emphasizing the human-animal bond and keeping families together.*

Guided by his philosophy that supporting people helps pets thrive, Wheeler has developed numerous community programs that enhance the lives of both people and pets. These initiatives have significantly reduced shelter intake while maintaining one of the lowest euthanasia rates in the region. At the same time, his programs have provided care and resources to thousands of families, underscoring his conviction that healthy pets are essential to building humane and resilient communities.

Wheeler's commitment to best practices and progressive animal services has earned him leadership roles on a national scale. He serves as Vice President of the National Animal Care and Control

Association, Treasurer and Past President of the Arkansas State Animal Control Association, and is a member of the Executive Management Committee for Human Animal Support Services (HASS). He also lends his expertise to numerous national advisory panels, shaping policy, training professionals, and guiding municipalities toward more effective and compassionate animal services.

Recognized internationally, Wheeler has shared his expertise at the Australian National Animal Welfare Conference (as Keynote Speaker), the Humane World for Animals Animal Care Expo (formerly sponsored by the Humane Society of the United States), the Best Friends Animal Society, and at state-level animal control and welfare associations nationwide.

Wheeler holds a Master of Business Administration with a minor in public administration, as well as a degree in Criminal Justice. A lifelong learner inspired by leaders in both human and animal welfare, he continues to evolve community support strategies that strengthen the bond between people and pets.

Together, these leaders show what is
possible when compassion shapes purpose.

What comes next is ours to carry forward.

www.PetPunditPublishing.com

www.ingramcontent.com/pod-product-compliance
Lightning Source LLC
LaVergne TN
LVHW012034100626
840935LV00049B/964
* 9 7 8 1 9 4 8 4 4 4 0 3 3 *